JACKSONVILLE Scavenger

Amy West

Reedy Press
PO Box 5131
St. Louis, MO 63139, USA
www.reedypress.com

Library of Congress Control Number: 2022937097

ISBN: 9781681063980

Cover and interior design by Claire Ford

Cover and interior photos by the author.
Interior clip art courtesy of Pixabay and Wikimedia Commons.

Printed in the United States of America
22 23 24 25 26 5 4 3 2 1

Dedication

For my Dad, Neal, who's always celebrated my mindset that any life experience can be seen as an adventure if you look at it from the right perspective.

encouragement you gave while I created this book. The days you spent driving me all over this giant city will be memories I carry with me forever as we rediscovered our big small town. Thank you for being as committed to the completion of this project as I have been. Your support has never wavered, nor did you complain as the laundry piled up and the house fell into disarray as I dropped everything to complete this book; you simply took up the extra shifts on top of the heavy load you already carry. I admire you so much and could not dream of a better partner.

Introduction

Welcome to the largest city by area in the continental United States. Jacksonville is full of experiences and in many ways feels like several cities united under one name. Each region has its own personality and subcultures. From the rural vibes of the Westside to the beaches and its laid-back attitude, you will find that the city and the rural areas have more in common here than they have differences. In fact, many people say that Jacksonville is the biggest small town you'll ever live in. Like most cities, Jacksonville natives have much civic pride, and it can be challenging to surprise them with something they don't know. After writing my first book, *100 Things to Do in Jacksonville Before You Die*, I received feedback both praising the surprises enclosed, and wishing to learn more of the secrets of our Bold City. In my explorations I have successfully uncovered an array of hidden gems and treasures I'm confident many will be delighted to explore. It's safe to say that some will find their own neighborhood clues will come to them comfortably; however, I think you'll find that solving over 300 clues spread throughout the city will become a thrilling challenge. So, whether you're solving these solo, or building your team, get ready to use this book as the key to unlock some of Jacksonville's greatest treasures.

Author's note: Although this book was intended ideally to include walkable routes, Jacksonville's vast spread and urban sprawl made that task difficult to accomplish. I have made notes in each neighborhood if they are walkable, drivable, or both. Please keep your safety in mind as you walk and drive through the city. Stay aware of your surroundings, and if you ever feel in danger, seek help immediately.

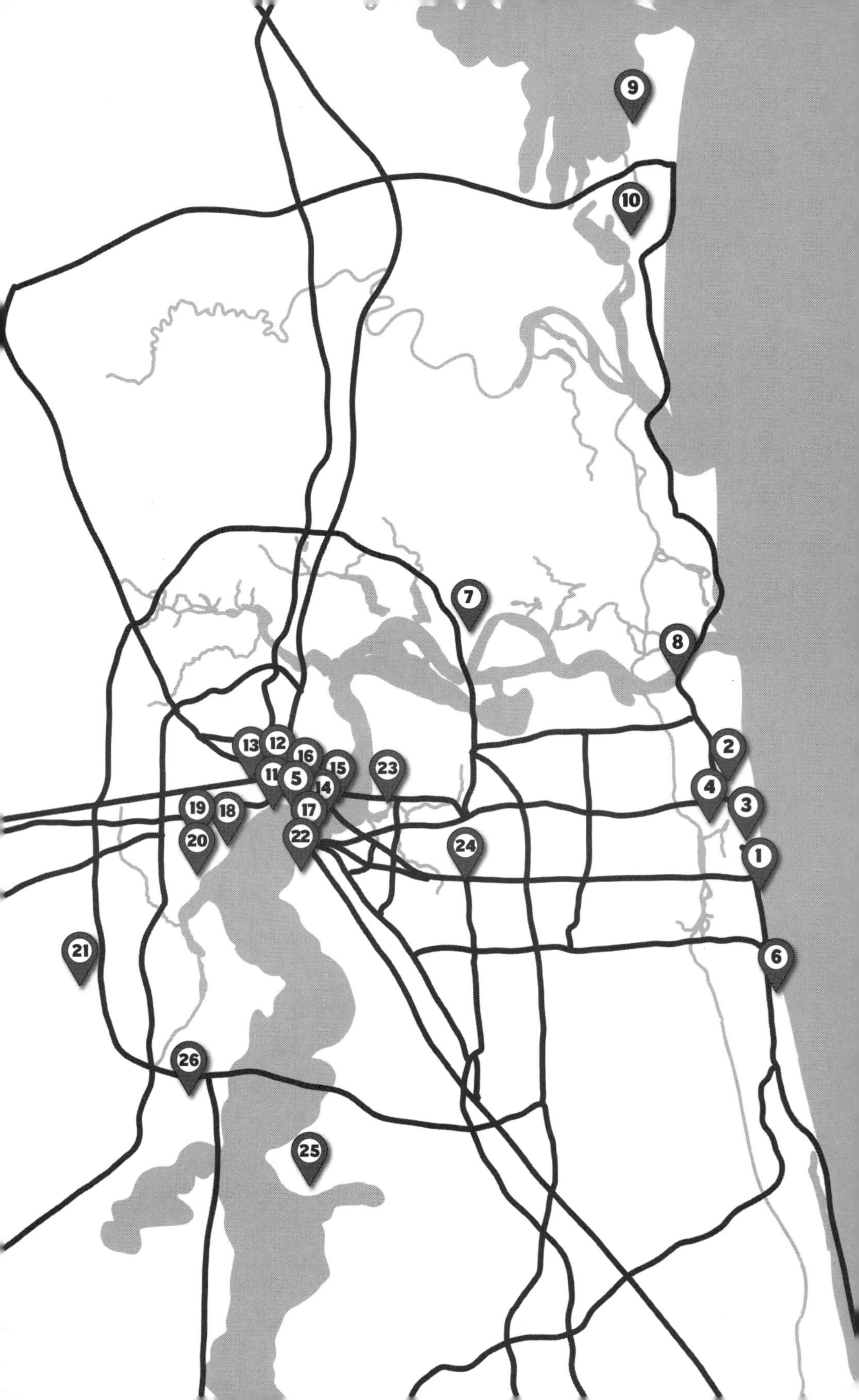
9
10
7
8
2
13
12
16
15
23
11
5
4
14
3
19
18
17
22
1
20
24
6
21
26
25

Legend

1 Jacksonville Beach
2 Atlantic Beach
3 Neptune Beach
4 Mayport
5 The Cultural Corridor
6 Ponte Vedra Beach
7 The Northside
8 Islands of Heckscher
9 Downtown Fernandina Beach
10 Amelia Island
11 Downtown
12 LaVilla
13 The Railyards
14 Sports District
15 The Shipyards
16 Springfield
17 Southbank
18 Riverside
19 Murray Hill
20 Avondale
21 Westside
22 San Marco
23 Arlington
24 Southside
25 Mandarin
26 Orange Park

Jacksonville Beach

Walk

As one of the four small towns that make up the beaches proper, Jacksonville Beach is perhaps the community's center point. Formerly known as Pablo Beach, the city's name was officially changed in 1925 to help identify the beach's location to potential visitors, while gaining more visibility nationally. Today, Jacksonville Beach is a vibrant community that draws visitors to its beautiful shoreline, casual nightlife, and easygoing beach lifestyle.

1

A hidden passage for locals only,
Spanning the marshlands, it's hardly lonely,
Belonging to monarchs only in name,
Connecting neighbors who went and who came.

2

If you need eggs or a bottle of wine,
At this convenient store, surely you'll find
That last ingredient or salty snack,
A tasty steak, or box of cheese and mac.

3

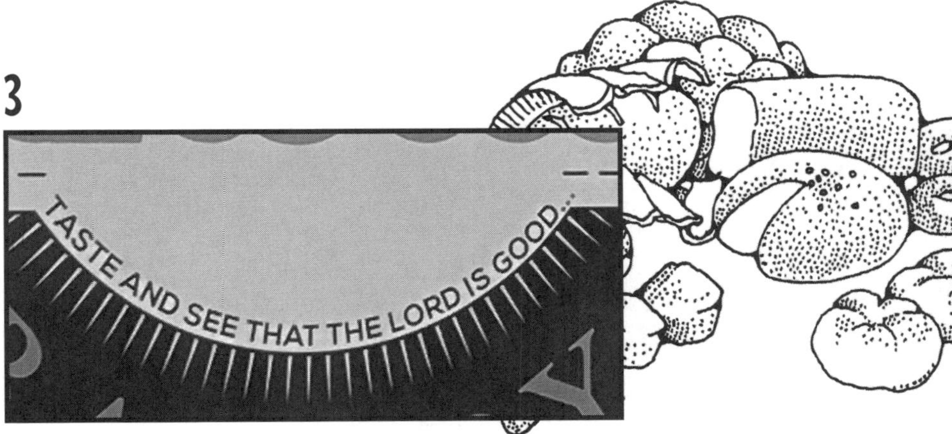

If you have a sweet tooth, and treats you crave,
Then your appetite you must truly save,
Wedding cakes, muffins, and cookies galore:
For pumpkin donuts, you will beg for more.

4

Look up and admire their evergreen heights
When peace and fresh air are on top of mind.
Pack up a picnic of savory bites:
The kids will explore, and you can unwind.

5

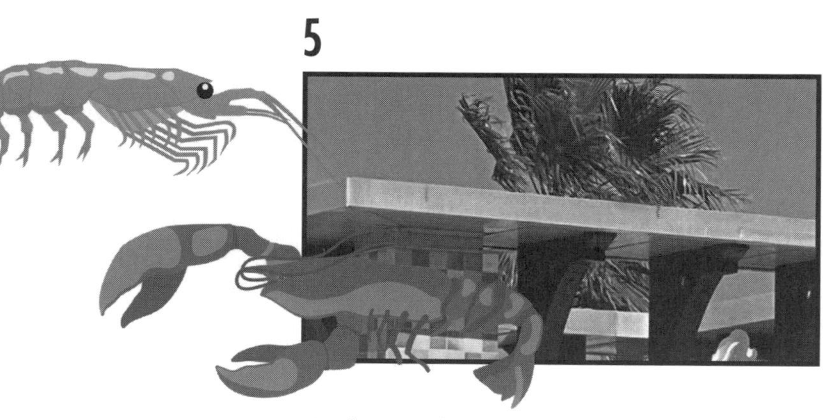

Embrace the beach culture with this cult brand
Known for their poke bowl, and tropic sips,
Their menu features meals from sea or land,
Handhelds, fresh catch, and of course, tasty dips.

If you're hungry, you might find yourself here
For a margarita, cocktail, or beer.
Cheeseburger in paradise, anyone?
Pass the salt shaker and join in the fun.

____

____

7

If walls could speak, then they'd tell stories
Of lively music, and bygone glories,
Celebrities were known to spend the night;
A view from the penthouse is quite the sight.

____

____

8

Rise and shine, go and grab some grub
For brunch or dinner at this pub,
Enjoy the ocean view and brew,
The fish and chips and live tunes, too.

9

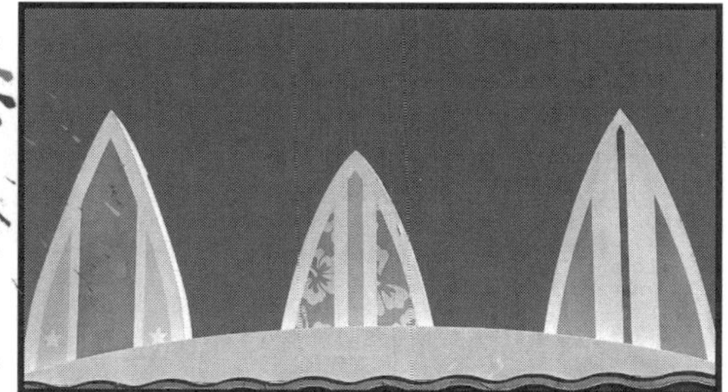

It stretches out into the sea,
Stroll over water and just be.
Cast a line and watch all the waves,
Current and tide, surfers do brave.

10

Where the community comes to unite,
The music and lights, indeed, are so bright
From spring through winter, here we celebrate
Open-air markets and concerts 'til late.

11

Its history has roots in southern rock,
If only its guests could turn back the clock,
Today it adds to the beaches' night scene,
A watering hole to see and be seen.

12

File your permits, or pay your bills:
It's all business, forget frills,
Taxes, rentals, and zoning rules,
Solve your problems or find the tools.

____

____

13

For over a century, they've stood guard,
Whether the job was easy or hard,
These volunteers could lend you their muscle.
Trouble in the water? They will hustle.

____

____

14

Legs for days, you will surely claim,
Straight from the ocean, they found fame.
Eat them with butter at this shack;
Without a doubt, you will be back.

15

A beaches figure, it's no mystery,
A place of worship full of history.
Relocated four times in the past,
Its charm and reverence through time will last.

16

Over 50 years without fail,
A place where words become full-scale,
The stories told here will delight
And imagination will take flight.

17

Mentoring green thumbs in training for years,
Educating, growing, and healing roots,
Enriching community friends and peers,
They do more than planting veggies and fruits.

18

At home, he guards the innocent creatures,
Before care, they must pass by his features,
Wings extended, he tries to alight;
Standing watch, he'll never take flight.

19

Gather the gang and head to this green space,
Hey, batter, batter, you better make base,
Slip down the slide with the greatest of ease:
Pack a picnic and enjoy the sea breeze.

20

They guard our shore with diligence,
Protect and serve each incidence,
A part of our courageous armed forces,
Safety of our coast it reinforces.

____

____

21

A secluded playground by the boatyard
You might just miss, unless you live local.
There is plenty of nature standing guard
Of this calm park by the intracoastal.

____

____

22

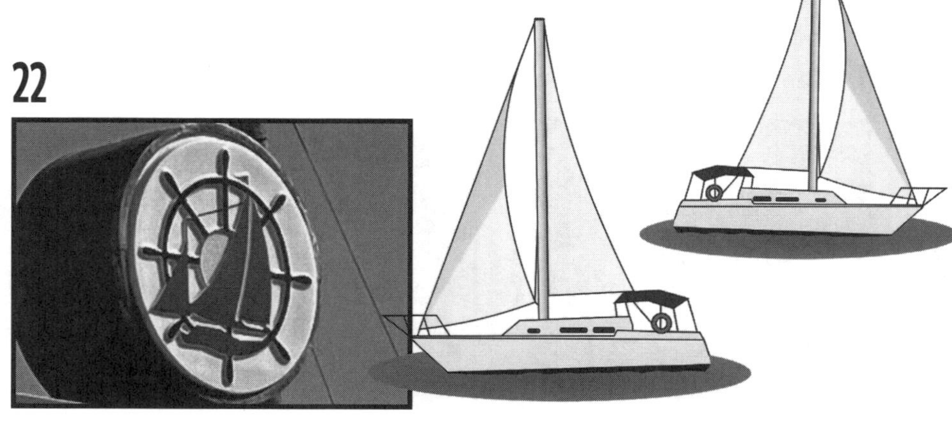

If you're a mariner, this might be home,
A place you'll launch from when you want to roam,
Sail, motor, speed, or catamarans,
You'll find them floating here, awaiting plans.

____

____

23

Legend says this restaurant is haunted,
Don't worry, your business is still wanted,
In the window or near the fireplace,
A shadow in the bathroom, a ghostly trace?

____

____

24

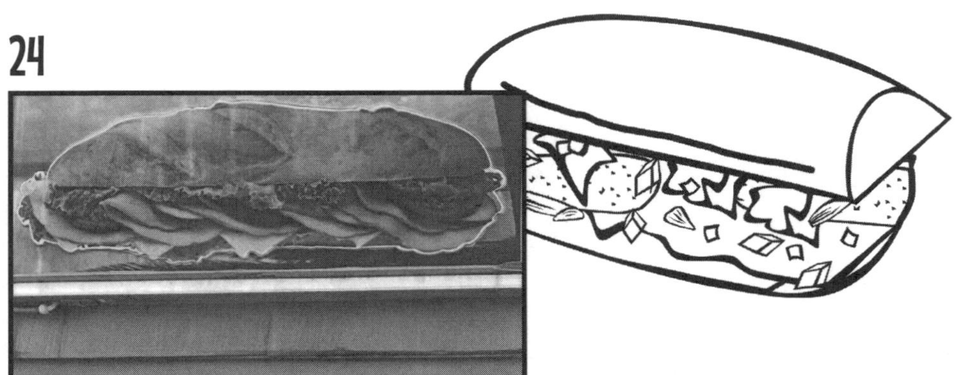

Housed in an old convenience store,
This place is in no way a bore.
Get it plain or with the sauce,
Order the crunchies, you're the boss.

25

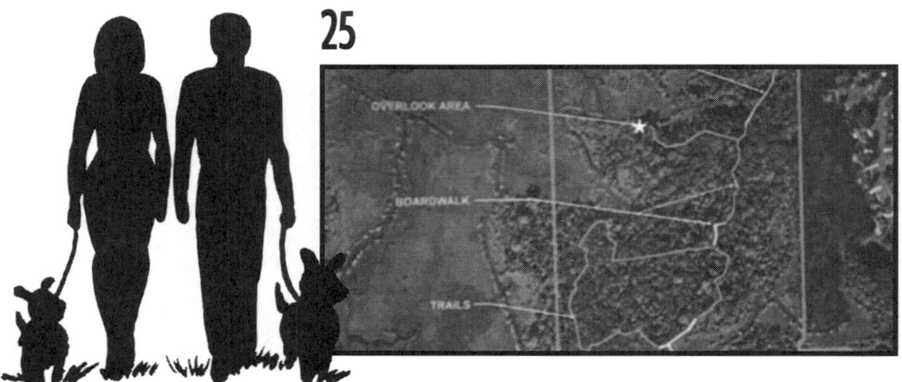

Wrapped in woodland hammock and marsh,
A stroll through this path isn't harsh,
Walk with your family or your dog,
Hike the path or go for a jog.

26

The favorite playground for man's best friend,
Big or small, energy they'll surely expend
Making new fur friends, and running some laps,
Don't be surprised if later they'll need naps.

27

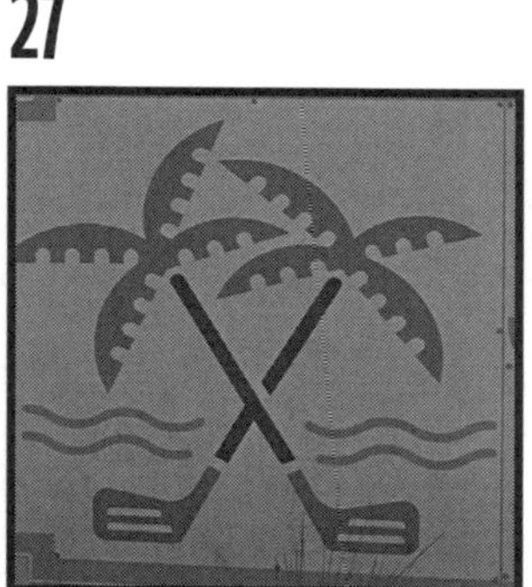

For 50-plus years this green has been played,
A beach's tradition, memories made,
Drive your ball or putt, sink, chip, score, and fly,
Lost in a trap? Then the ball you must spy.

28

For over a century they've had rest
Here in the center of the beach's heart,
Cared for by its namesake, he did his best
To honor the Black deceased, for his part.

____

____

29

Inspired by the surf and sand,
This publisher brings a new brand,
Getting crafty here at the beach,
Expanding minds and flavors' reach.

____

____

30

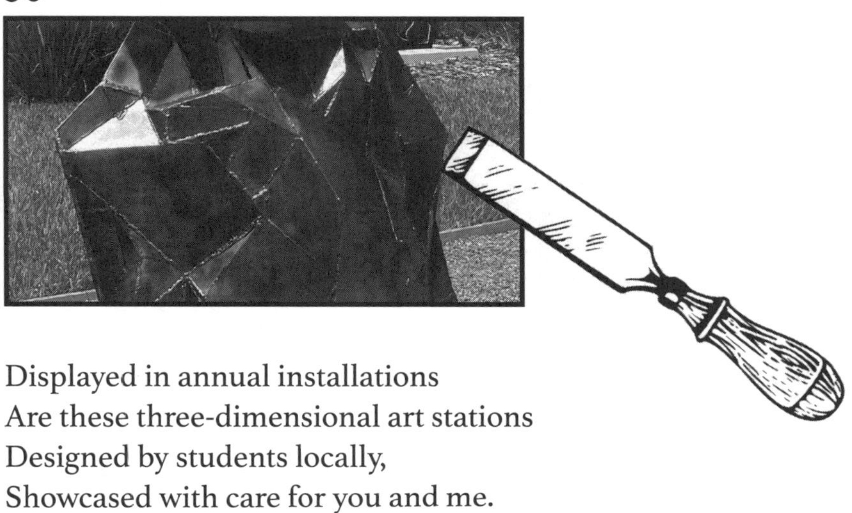

Displayed in annual installations
Are these three-dimensional art stations
Designed by students locally,
Showcased with care for you and me.

____

____

31

Can you see him smile with glee
As he rides astride the sea?
Gliding along with noble steed,
All for future youth he'll lead.

____

____

32

A sip of wine and new friends at the bar,
A walk to the shoreline wouldn't be far,
Wood-fired delicacies, and dessert, too,
The guest list reads like a social who's-who.

33

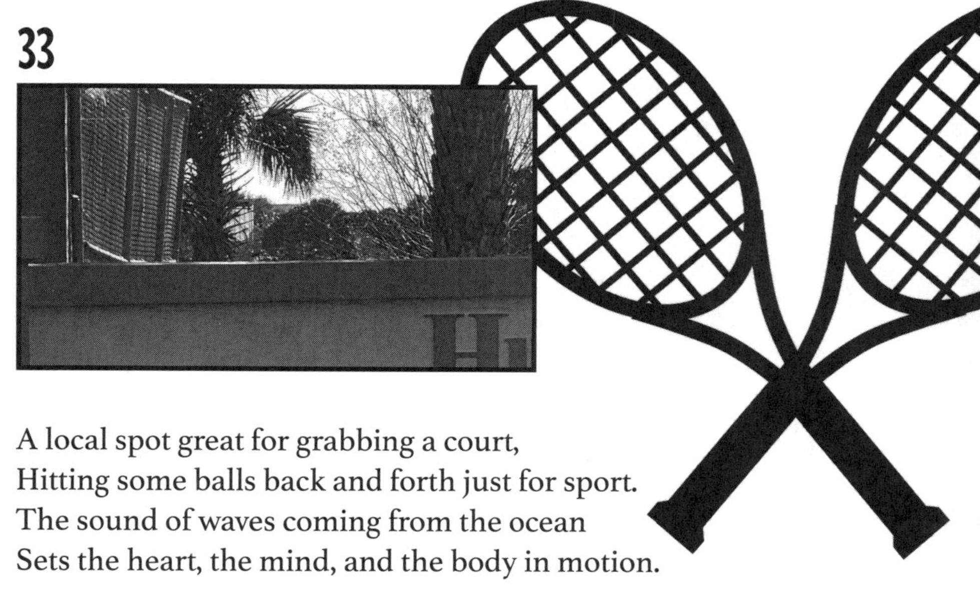

A local spot great for grabbing a court,
Hitting some balls back and forth just for sport.
The sound of waves coming from the ocean
Sets the heart, the mind, and the body in motion.

34

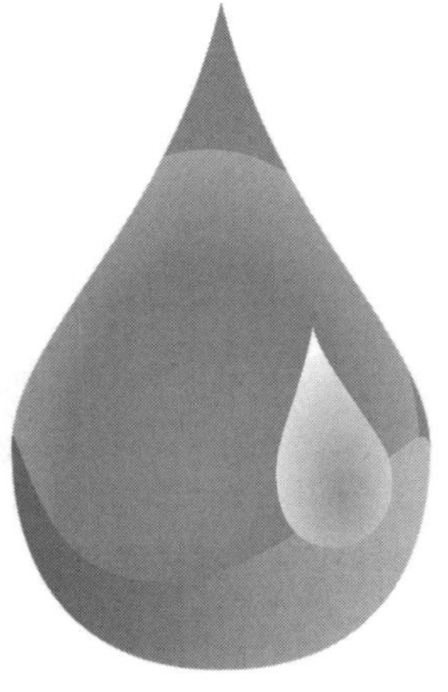

A lifeguard stand displayed on its belly,
This belly isn't one that's full of jelly,
Instead, its tank's filled with H2O,
A treasure to the suburb it will flow.

35

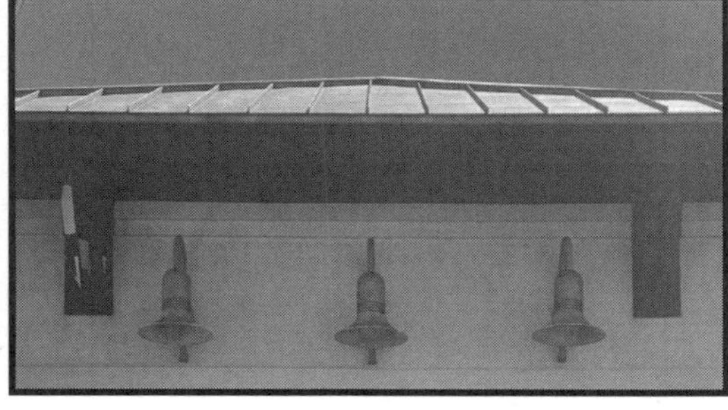

Named for the moniker of the city,
As strong as its brew and twice as pretty,
Gather together associates and friends,
Taste the sweet delicacies of its blends.

Atlantic Beach and Neptune Beach

Walk

Atlantic Beach and Neptune Beach converge in the Beaches Town Center, with half of the shopping center in Atlantic Beach and half in Neptune Beach. Although they are intimately acquainted, each has its own distinct personality and subculture. Atlantic Beach houses extraordinary, high-end beach homes alongside charming cottages in a heavily wooded, shoreside community. You'll find plenty of green space, stylish boutiques, and fine dining, as well as a bustling art scene. Neptune Beach is a bit more buttoned up on its residential side, still featuring great restaurants and shops, but encourages its residents to keep reasonable hours, drive the speed limit, and enjoy the great outdoors.

1

A cozy corner in Atlantic Beach,
A peaceful moment that is here for each
Child or adult who might meander by:
Take a deep breath, and just gaze at the sky.

2

Here for a social engagement or green,
A place the who's-who can see and be seen,
For an active social life it's meant,
Swim in the pool or join a fun event.

____

____

3

An Atlantic Beach best-kept-secret haunt,
A local fave when you're out for a jaunt,
A place you'll collect both the sun and shade,
Forget all your worries and have it made.

____

____

4

Art on display and music to be heard,
A gathering space for the spoken word.
Have your work meeting here or a party,
Rent this space and they'll think you're a smarty.

5

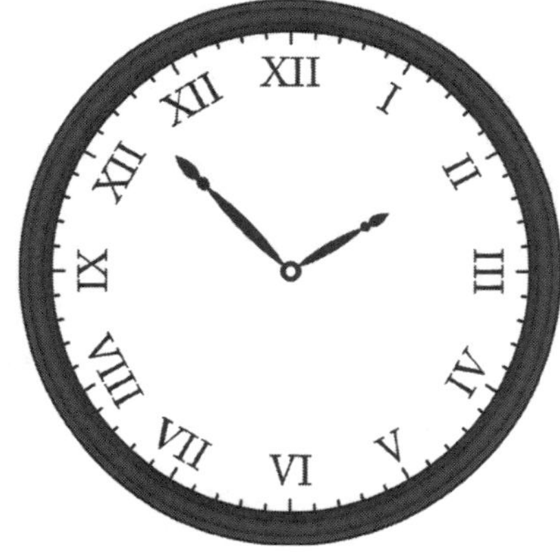

Five roads converge here, and cars wait their turn,
No time to waste or extra gas to burn,
Measure the seconds as they tick on by,
When you look up, you'll see how fast they fly.

6

Call up the gang and don't forget your board,
In this concrete jungle you could be lord,
Go for a wall ride, fakie, or board slide,
Wear your helmet and practice with pride.

7

A hidden cove full of outdoor treasures,
Special events here are fresh-air pleasures,
Observe nature or walk the trails,
The open-air life sure can heal what ails.

8

Here the bell rings, as if saying "go home,"
The kids at their desk will put down their tomes,
Picked up by their parents in long car lines,
Riding on buses past "go slowly" signs.

____

____

9

A hip retreat that's so close to the beach,
Remade and reclaimed into something sweet,
Hit the waves, or walk to the town center,
You'll relax here the moment you enter.

____

____

10

Once for entertainment, now for reverence,
The temple for big-screen stars, now for God,
What once was revered, served its severance,
A transformed space for sacred praises laud.

11

Rub off a little Emerald Isle luck here,
Grab a few friends and have a beer,
The sister owners can throw a party;
You'll feel like family and eat hearty.

12

Once known to the locals as the Sea Turtle,
Converting this space was quite the hurdle,
Now luxury lives here among the dunes,
Fine dining and romance will be your boon.

____

____

13

This iconic watering hole is known
For great eats, and the nightlife it has grown,
Dance your cares away to the tunes and beat,
While Cajun-inspired fare you will eat.

____

____

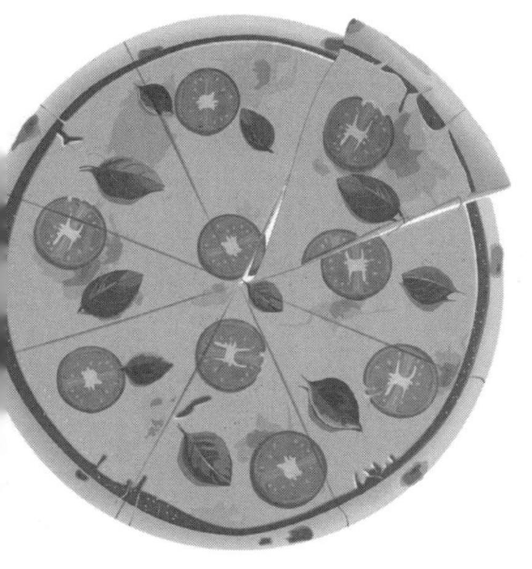

14

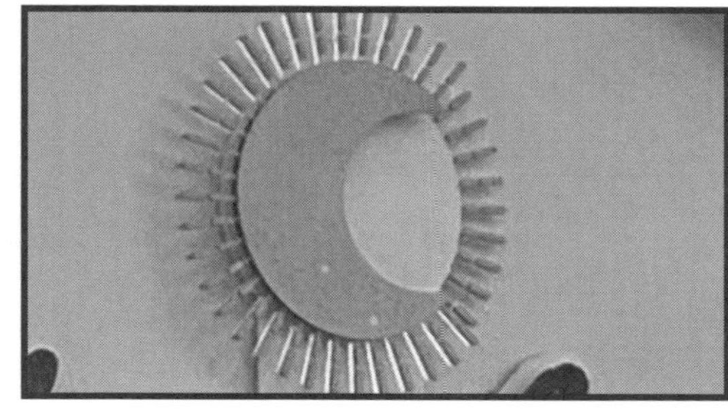

Wood-fired pizza, cocktails, and wine,
Romantic atmosphere that's quite divine,
Don't forget to make a reservation
At this Italian beach sensation.

15

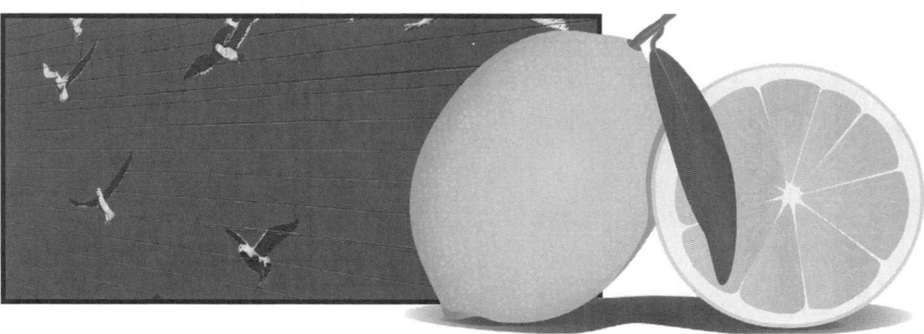

Dubbed for the sour fruit on a citrus tree,
This watering hole is the place to be,
Bring your ID or you may not get through
To enjoy a delicious beachside brew.

16

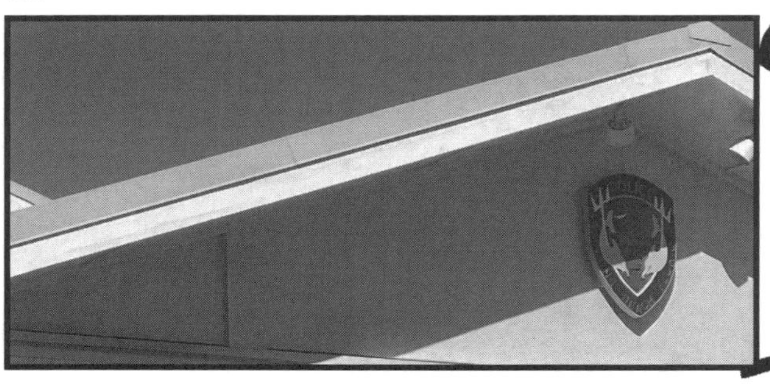

Mind your manners and watch your speed
When in conflict or if help you need,
Keeping a friendly watch for you
Are these superheroes in blue.

17

A cup of joe or a glass of fine wine,
Hang with your friends when the weather is fine,
Available Wi-Fi for working remote,
Man's best friend is welcome, so take note.

18

On their sign sits a fabulous pink bird,
Famous for saltwater dining, I've heard,
Eat alfresco or choose to dine inside,
Newly updated and full of beach pride.

19

In need of the latest hot summer read,
Or perhaps it's a mystery novel you need?
Find plenty of tomes here for your browsing:
You'll discover a read that's arousing.

20

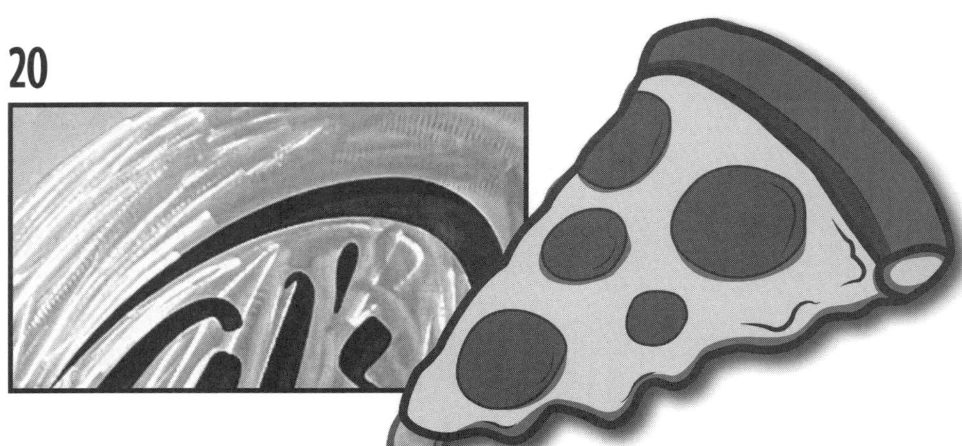

Mama mia, it's time for pie,
Watch it hand-tossed up to the sky.
Care for some bread or a spicy meatball?
The menu has something for one and for all.

____

____

21

Admire its spire, soaring up so high,
The doors are open for all to come by.
Offer a prayer in this sacred space,
All are welcome and belong in this place.

____

____

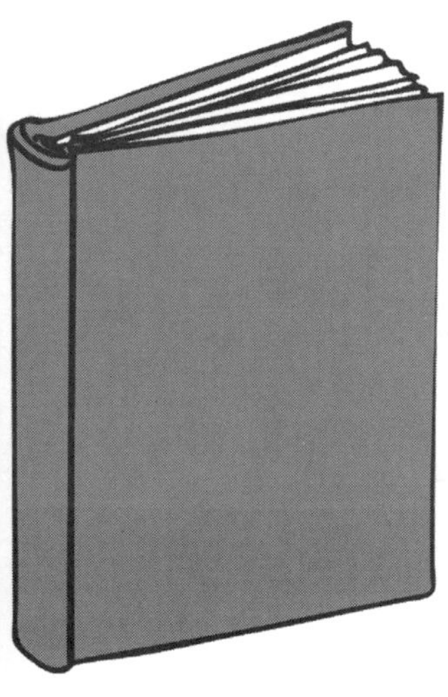

22

Find your research and finish your paper,
Gather some insight in this mind shaper,
The Dewey decimal system's your friend,
If, in the stacks, it's time you'll need to spend.

23

Pickleball, tennis, and basketball, too,
Peaceful gardens and walking paths for you,
Climb up the ropes, and slip-slip down the slide,
Your fun options in this green space are wide.

The Cultural Corridor

Walk

Due to the industrial nature of this neighborhood, please keep safety your priority.

The Cultural Corridor is zoned as part of Atlantic Beach, yet embraces a distinctive personality of its own. A growing destination for up-and-coming breweries and distilleries, the Cultural Corridor is akin to the Wynwood entertainment district of Miami, Florida. Take a selfie tour of the colorful murals, explore an oceanside park, grab some grub from a hip food truck, and embrace the revival taking place in this once-distressed neighborhood.

1

Grab your best fur friend and jump in the car,
Fun for you and your dog isn't too far,
On the AstroTurf he'll run, jump, and play,
For drinks with friends, you'll want to stay.

2

For a refreshing evening walk,
Enjoy the sunset while you talk,
Head to the intracoastal side,
Let the lovely path be your guide.

3

Find your next local-made treasure here,
So many talented artists, it's clear,
Sign up for classes to enhance your skills,
Here, you'll have plenty of artistic thrills.

4

A little piece of Wynwood here in Jax,
For color and design, it has no lack,
You might just find your next great selfie op
If you really want those photos to pop.

____

____

5

With over 60 years of history,
It's reputation is no mystery,
Affordable drinks and a light-up floor,
The food and pool will have you wanting more.

____

____

6

When the kids have too much spirit,
Head to this playground and clear it,
Swing, balance, run, and even hide,
Go up the stairs, and down the slide.

7

A natural hidden gem to explore,
Camp, hike, or fish, and still there's more
To see and do out in the wild,
Whether you're an adult or child.

Mayport

Walk

Nestled between the St. Johns River and Mayport Naval Station, the historic town of Mayport is both charming and intimate. Situated directly on the famous State Road A1A, this working fishing village is known for the shrimping vessels that flank its shoreline. Make sure to grab some wild-caught shrimp while you're in the neighborhood, and learn about Mayport's diverse marine history.

1

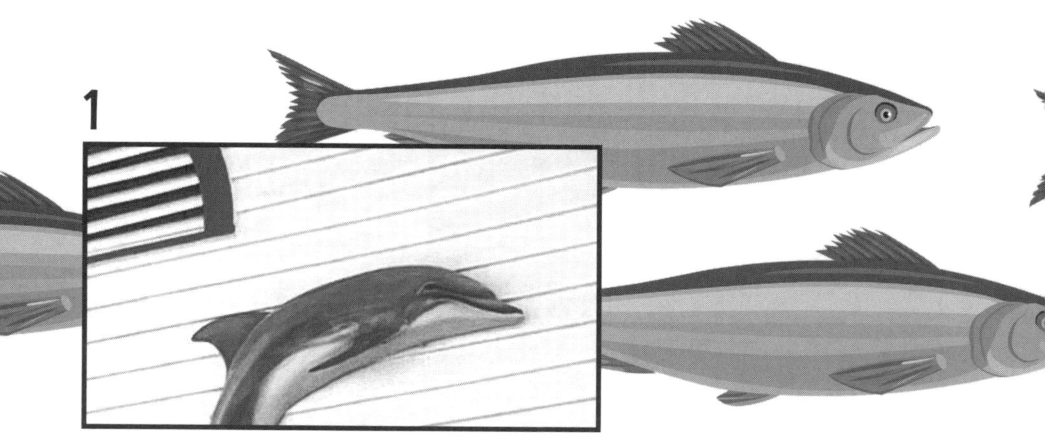

Marine biologists in the making
Come and soak up knowledge for the taking,
Making scientific observations
Of marine life for their education.

2

You'll find this sign in the village's heart,
It's the place where you should start,
Explore the hamlet's history and lore,
From its famed beacon to the rocky shore.

___

___

3

This old signal keeps our sailors aware
Of any dangers to be found out there.
Moved once and restored to former glory,
Through currents and time, it tells its story.

___

___

4

A quiet and peaceful house of prayer
When you need to know someone is there
To lend an ear or some consolation,
No matter your lifestyle or your station.

5

Jax has many ways to cross the water,
Whether you're solo or with your daughter.
You'll cross the St. Johns River with ease
On this most scenic route: it's a breeze.

6

The ocean's apex predator they track,
Whether swimming afar or hunting snacks,
They tag and name the water's fiercest fish,
So valuable data they do not miss.

7

When it's the harvest of the sea you crave,
You should head to one of the locals' faves,
Fish, crab, oysters, and wild-caught shrimp,
Come with a big appetite, and don't skimp.

8

If for seafood you would shop,
This is the place you have to stop
For the freshest saltwater fare,
Plenty for you, and some to share.

____

____

9

Always ready is their precept,
Out of boats and helos they've leapt,
Saving lives and guarding borders,
Waiting bravely for their orders.

____

____

10

Access to this side isn't as preferred
As the main entrance for most of the herd,
To pass through you must have your entry card
Or risk rejection by the sentry guard.

11

This park is known by two different names,
You're an expert if you discern both claims,
Known for its natural seawall of rocks,
Not too far from the fishermen's boat docks.

Ponte Vedra Beach

Drive

Home of THE PLAYERS Championship, Ponte Vedra Beach has a cultured history the locals are proud of. Stately homes rest on well-manicured lawns in this coastal community, where golf courses frame most neighborhoods. If you're hungry for delicious seafood, or in search of shark teeth, you'll find both on the pristine coastline of Ponte Vedra Beach.

1

Families have stayed for generations,
One of the most beloved in the nation
For its beach, and the hospitality,
Friendly staff, and its luxe mentality.

2

A hidden treasure tucked away,
Here you can meditate and play,
Wandering paths round a peaceful lake,
A regular retreat of this, you'll make.

3

Amazing views and the freshest of fare,
A friendly, knowing staff that cares,
Southern favorite dishes and gorgeous views,
It's always sunshine here, never the blues.

A luxury abode on a famous course,
If you want a retreat, then try this source,
Fine dining and cocktails for your next stay,
Or how 'bout a spa day, whadda you say?

5

Golf's big competitions have a new home:
From this modern building, it takes its throne
To organize and execute the games
Where players turn legends, and rise to fame.

6

Families rest here amongst the deceased,
Slumbering forever in final peace
Under the shade of ancient Southern oaks
With generations of departed folk.

7

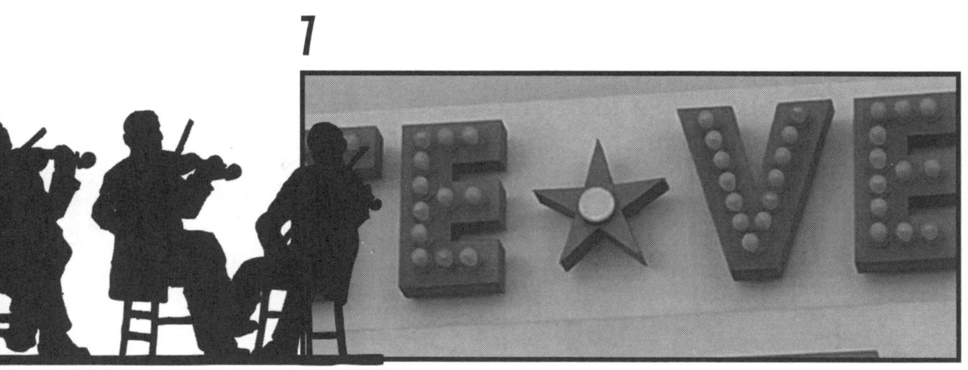

From hymnals to encores this space evolved,
Rock legends and comics and all involved
Have graced this humble place with their glamour,
All for the crowd's applause and clamor.

8

Ponte Vedra's first public beach,
Through the shelly sand you will reach
The water's edge, so warm on toes,
Framed by opulent homes, it flows.

9

If you didn't know it was there, you'd miss
The cawing of birds or exotic hiss,
Your extravaganza will be quite wild
For every adult or curious child.

10

The back entrance to this sanctuary
Is lesser-known, but not at all scary,
Go for a hike, or bike beside creatures,
Birds, boar, and cats are some of its features.

The Northside and the Islands of Heckscher

Drive

The Northside of Jacksonville is vast, and home to much industrial and maritime business. It also houses some of the First Coast's most beautiful historic and ecological treasures. Along your explorations you'll observe rural farms, large factories, and expansive forests.

The road trip up Heckscher Drive is one of the most scenic in Jacksonville. Stretching through several barrier reef islands, Heckscher Drive gets you up-close and personal with the historical timeline of the First Coast. From plantations to shrimp boats, and ruins dating back almost two centuries, you'll get a glimpse into the past, where evidence of human occupation dates back over 5,000 years!

1

It the longest of its kind in the States,
Its shape is unique, like entering gates,
If you have vertigo, do not look down;
Instead, look at the scenic view of town.

2

In the shade of the span, a small retreat,
A corner to fish or to have a seat,
A place to remember those lost at sea,
For the present, that is, and what could be.

3

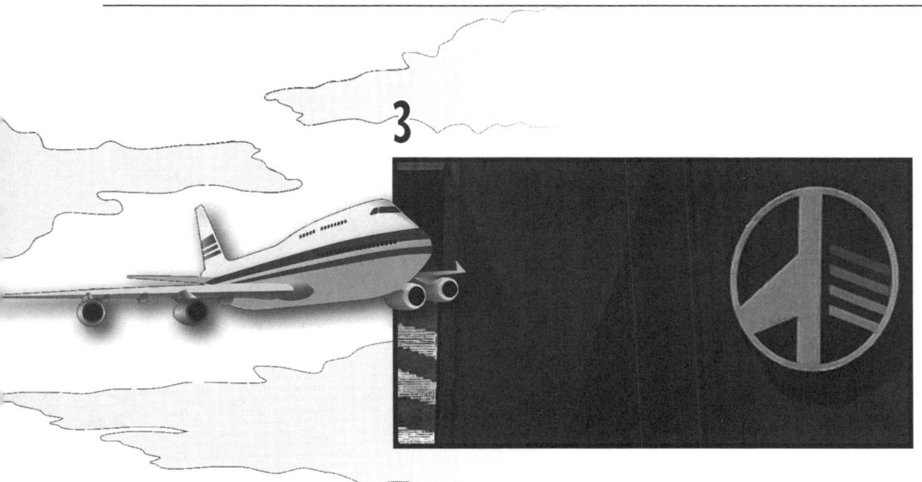

Need an adventure or a getaway?
Discover the transport you need to stray.
There is nothing to fear: let your soul soar!
From up here, you can see all that's in store.

4

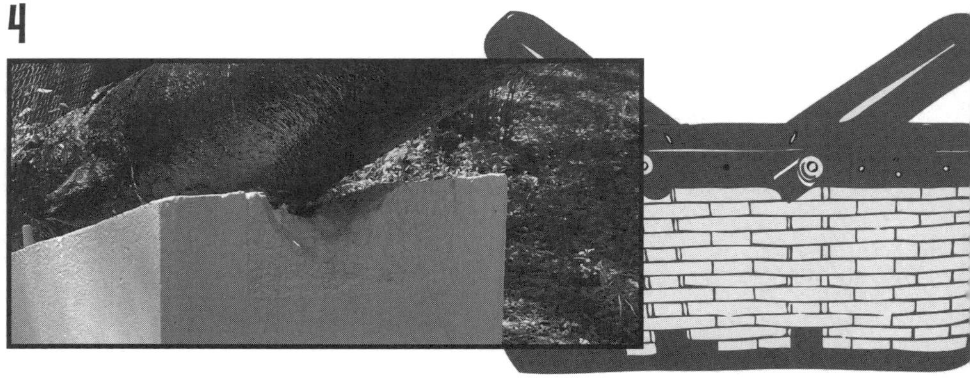

A strategic site in the Civil War
For defending the coast in time before,
Today, you can picnic or take a walk,
Listen to bees buzz, and birds squawk.

5

Voted one of the best in the nation,
It's a must-see if you're on vacation,
You won't need to skip the little brick road
To see lions, tigers, bears . . . and toads.

6

Voted number-one thing to do in Jax
When your wilder side wants to feel its max,
Visit the residents for a night feed,
Keep your hands to yourself, or you might bleed.

____

____

7

A forgotten ground once hallowed,
Lost amongst the town that followed,
The ways of old times gone before
Along this village by the shore.

____

____

8

Fancy a tractor ride at dusk?
Then a visit here is a must.
Sip on their cider while you dine,
See if the mayhaws you can find.

9

A place for our bravest to be at rest,
It's most peaceful here, no place for stress,
Receive the honors your courage has earned:
Not all our heroes wear capes, we have learned.

10

Taking our Jax hops to a whole new scale:
If craft is a fish, then this is a whale,
One of twelve locales across these great states,
A cold one and happy hour are best mates.

11

One man's trash can be a treasure,
Only a keen eye can measure,
750 stalls are here,
When you find your prize, you will cheer.

12

When it's time to stock up on supplies,
Grab coffee, burger, or maybe fries,
Head to this popular Northside center,
Window-shop outside or a store enter.

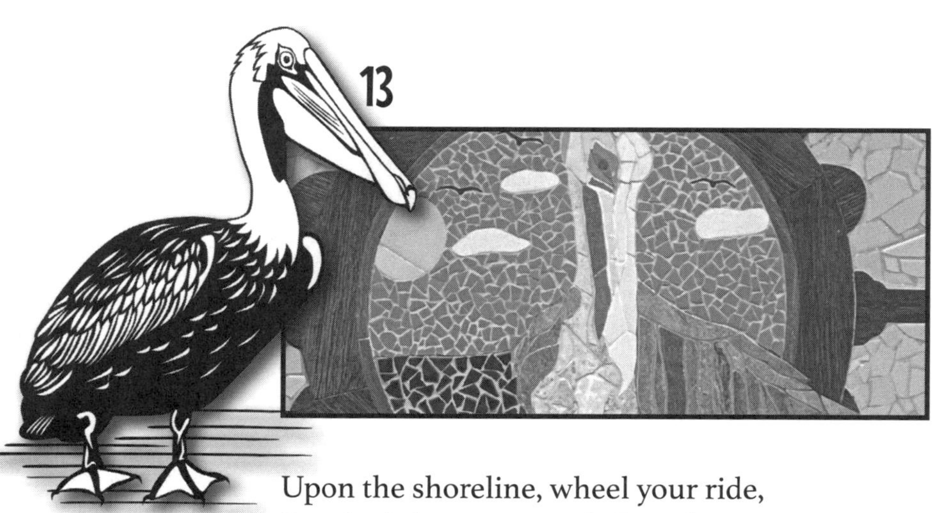

13

Upon the shoreline, wheel your ride,
But don't forget to watch the tide,
The waves do have an appetite
For metal, rubber, and headlights.

14

It's the oldest surviving in the state
From a time that once was controlled by hate.
We can chose to learn from this era past,
Don't repeat history: let's make change last.

15

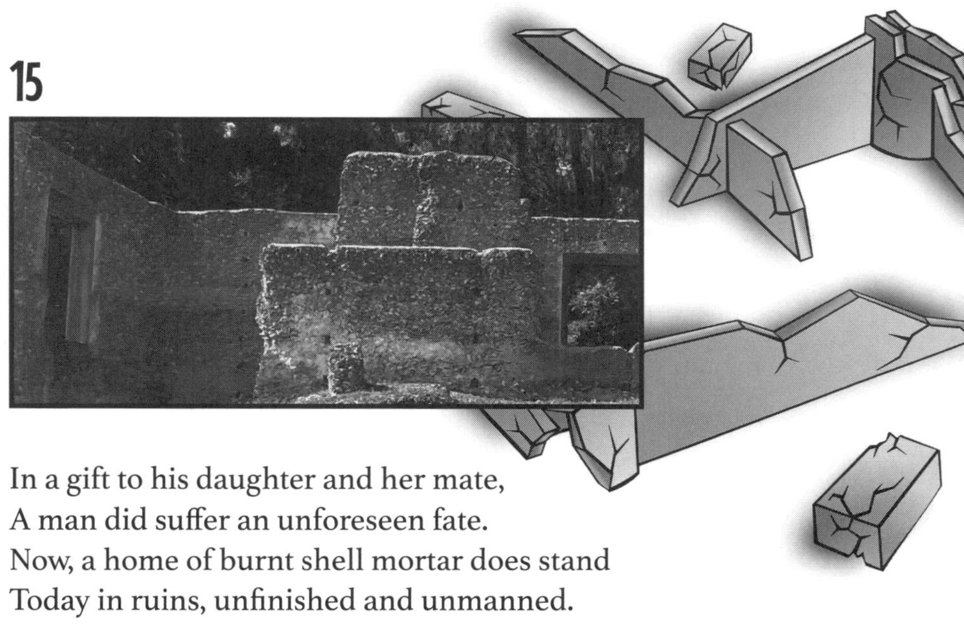

In a gift to his daughter and her mate,
A man did suffer an unforeseen fate.
Now, a home of burnt shell mortar does stand
Today in ruins, unfinished and unmanned.

16

Named for the first explorer to lay claim,
Elegant in history and in name,
A resort for the rich in the '20s,
Now, they hold stunning weddings aplenty.

17

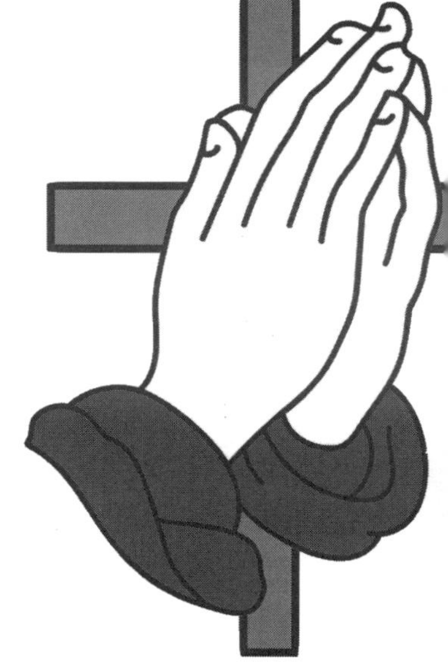

Built in timeless carpenter Gothic style,
Gatherers enter red doors with a smile,
Here to worship on this historic isle,
Receive a blessing and stay for a while.

18

This small barrier reef island's not big;
The sweet baby turtles who hatch here zig
Back and forth 'til they reach the ocean waves,
Or, when they're in peril, a caring soul saves.

Downtown Fernandina Beach

Walk/Drive

Fernandina Beach has also been called the Isle of Eight Flags. No other place in the United States can claim that. This historical diversity has created a unique culture in Fernandina Beach, which has many remarkable stories to tell, from pirates to patriots! Enjoy a stroll through downtown Fernandina Beach's charming Centre Street, where you'll discover quaint boutiques, delectable dining, and popular outdoor events, such as Dickens on Centre each December and the annual Isle of Eight Flags Shrimp Festival in the spring.

1

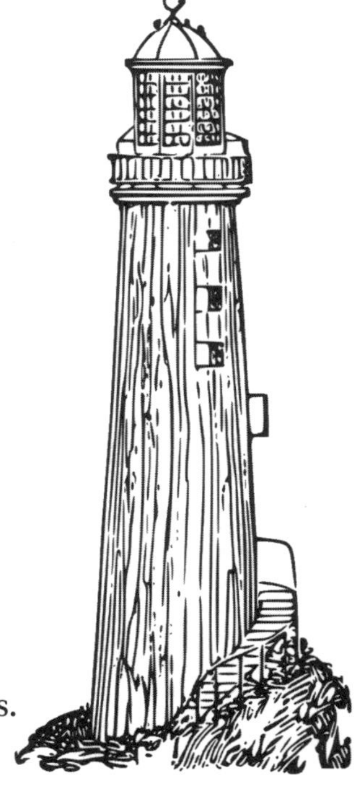

At the highest point of the Isle it stands,
Oldest in the state to weather the sands,
Guiding vessels from up to 15 miles,
Thus, countless have been kept away from trials.

2

This fortress served in three major conflicts.
For its strategic position, it was picked,
Today, you can kayak, hike, or explore,
Relive history from its gates to shore.

3

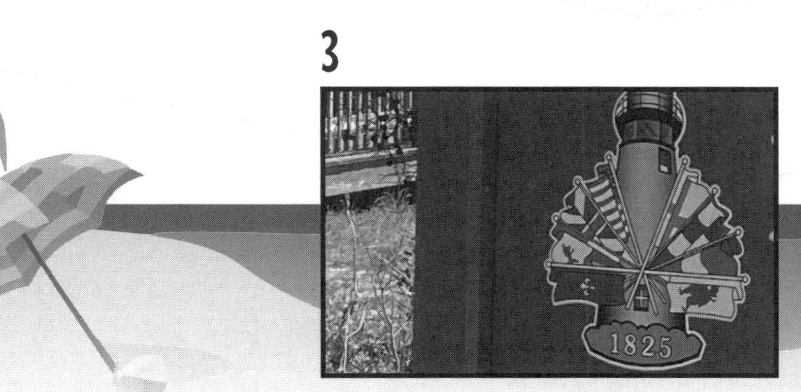

For a quiet escape by the seashore,
Plan to head north and explore even more,
This intimate retreat welcomes all to rest,
Stretch out on the sands and let go of stress.

4

Run free and let chaos ensue,
Pass the time when there's naught to do,
Grab your crew and yell, "Yo, Ho Ho!"
This sea on land lets young minds grow.

____

____

5

Out of the Hamptons, it looks like it came
Holding court on the sands, like a grande dame,
Stay for a night in her tasteful embrace,
Where every room offers plenty of space.

____

____

6

Over 300 acres to wander,
Ride, walk, hike, or just sit and ponder.
This protected landscape will beckon you
With its marsh so green, and its sky so blue.

7

They say we all have a book we could write,
Yet few can rarely get over the fight.
Here, you'll be inspired by what is inside,
Find a new read, and let the masters guide.

8

Spoken word and docent-driven,
Storytelling is their mission.
A building used for confinement
Now holds treasure that time has sent.

9

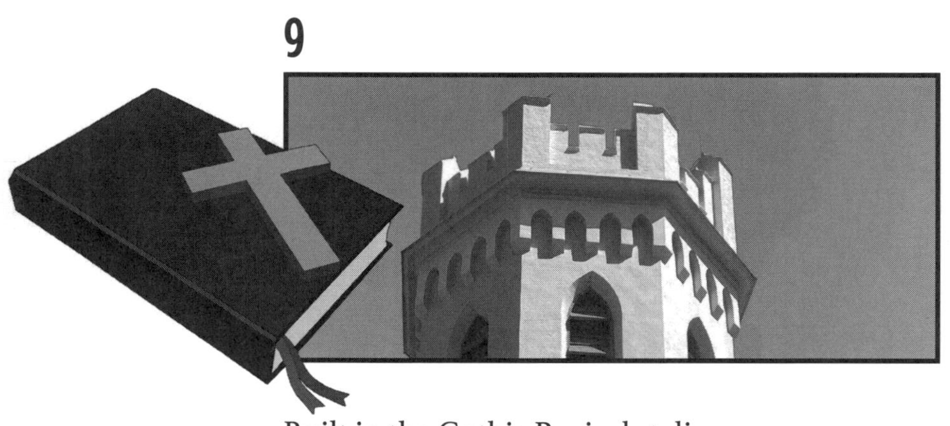

Built in the Gothic Revival styling,
The look of a castle it's profiling,
One of the oldest churches in the town
If you're in the Centre of things it's around.

10

The Captain once did here reside
And watch the boats come in on the tide,
Then a little red-haired girl came
And Hollywood was never the same.

11

Housed in a former train station,
Helping you plan your vacation
Under the eight flags that have flown,
Informed by people who have known.

12

The oldest shop in town for worms to dive,
It's here a well-crafted story does thrive,
"Old-fashioned" for us is a compliment,
"They don't make it like that," its achievement.

13

If in the center of things you would dock,
From here you can see what you want and walk,
Boutiques, entertainment, shops, and dining,
This place has everything for which you are pining.

14

Discover the spirit that pirates craved,
Along with vodka and cello, they braved
Creating small-batch classics from the heart,
Perhaps at a tasting you'd like to start.

15

A purposeful mission and aesthetic,
A craft statement unapologetic,
Found by the big water where the sun's born,
You will like it here: you won't be torn.

16

The oldest watering hole in the state,
Where service and cocktails are top-rate,
From shoes to booze, the orders did evolve,
Many a problem a bartender solved.

17

The oldest to survive inside the state,
A reason to visit and celebrate,
If you love history, you'll get your fill,
It's like sleeping in a real time capsule.

18

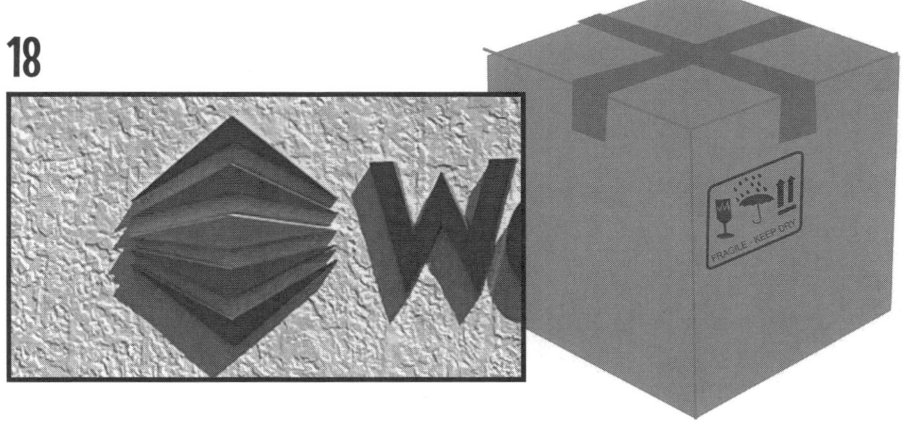

When your package comes from the online store,
Where is the box made? How do they get more?
On this small island, the answer does lie,
Look out for the stacks as you pass it by.

19

Once a fort did take up arms here
And natives also camped in the clear.
Today, you can rest and enjoy the space,
Look at the water with sun on your face.

20

This stately residence you must go see,
To unlock history, this is the key,
They don't make them like this anymore,
An example of building from before.

21

If you'd like to borrow a read,
Let the staff here take the lead,
Find a corner and cozy in,
Let your research or work begin.

A historical gem, this building is
Now a place to do some biz,
Take a class or listen to tunes,
Let your mind expand like balloons.

23

The oldest occupied home on the isle,
If houses could talk, perhaps they would smile
And tell the tale of five generations,
Where changes did come for sons and nations.

This historic building is prominent,
Its bell tower stands out, dominant,
Its Corinthian columns are stately;
If you walk by, you'll be impressed greatly.

____

____

25

In need of handling a city matter?
Taxes or permits? Let's do the latter,
Easy to find in the middle of town,
We'll make it quick, you don't need to frown.

____

____

26

If it's a package you'd like to mail,
Into this old building you'll have to sail.
Over 100 years it has conveyed
All the communication you have paid.

Amelia Island

Drive

Although Fernandina Beach is technically located on Amelia Island, most residing here distinguish it separately. For this reason, I have given the rest of the island its own section, as it certainly enjoys a distinct personality of its own. Outside of the small historic town of Fernandina Beach, Amelia Island becomes a haven of retreat, where luxurious resorts frame the shoreline in quiet reflection. Families ride bikes along ancient, preserved seaside forests, and things move just a bit slower here, in the epitome of Southern luxury.

1

For over 30 years this icon stands,
Stately and award-winning on these sands,
Known for its luxury and top service,
You'll relax here, and never be nervous.

2

Tennis, golf, nature, and beauty,
All the luxury, none of the snooty,
Southern hospitality at its best,
Embracing nature with vigor and zest.

3

In a world still locked in segregation,
There was a dream and determination,
One man built a fine seaside getaway
For African Americans to visit and play.

4

A favorite local seafood joint
With a stunning ocean viewpoint,
Sit at the bar where they have swings!
The tasty drinks will give you wings.

5

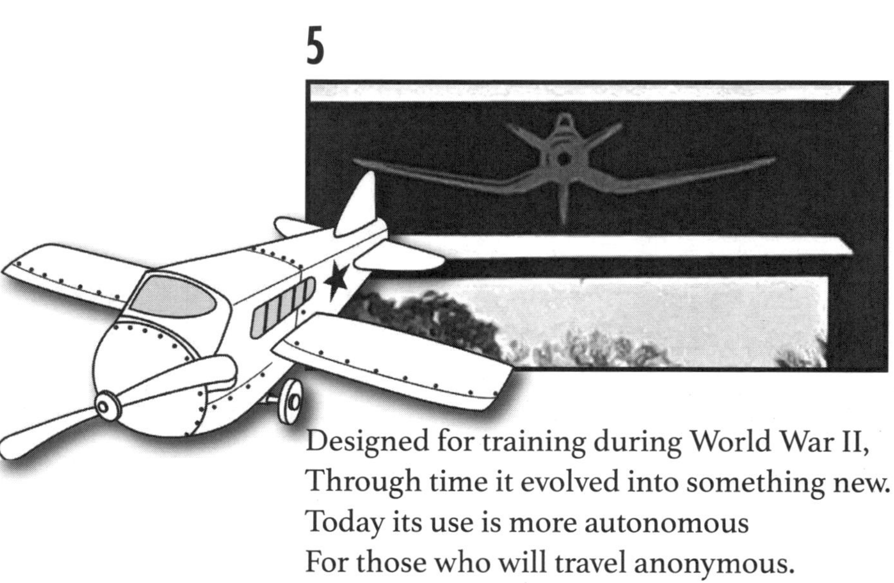

Designed for training during World War II,
Through time it evolved into something new.
Today its use is more autonomous
For those who will travel anonymous.

6

Here's the tallest sand dune in the state,
On a rare, special beach it has its fate,
Named by the beach lady who worked and cared,
Protected the dune and made sure it fared.

7

200-plus acres of land are here,
You can roam and walk, no need to fear,
Ride a horse or simply sunbathe and be,
Take a hike and explore here by the sea.

8

There are more creative ways to explore,
If this island you would like to see more,
One can take a bike, Segway, or a kart:
It's the most unique way for you to start.

9

Over 3,000 miles are on this great path,
If you rode it all, you might need a bath,
From Maine to Florida you can make way,
You can beat the record, or stay and play.

10

Fancy a visit with a wild local?
Talk to the naturalist, they'll be vocal.
They'll guide you through the natural trailheads,
You can hike, kayak, or go fishing, instead.

11

Come alone or attend with a friend,
At the Plantation, a fine time you'll spend,
A new ritual you will find:
A massage equals peace of mind.

12

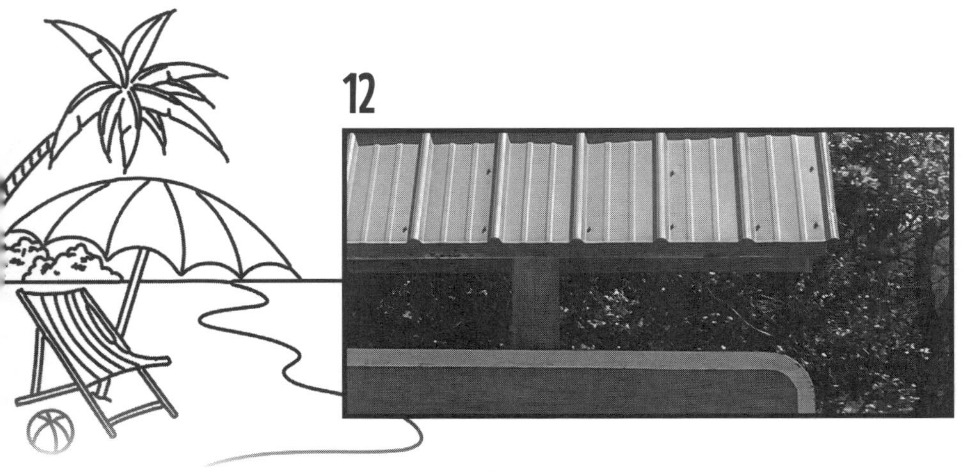

At home where American Beach once sat,
Now, where a peaceful getaway is at,
Access the natural wonder of the sands,
Soak up the sun, feel the grains in your hands.

13

An old tradition is restored anew,
Welcoming the many, not just the few,
Cast for tarpon, whiting, or drum,
With a catch or not, you'll still have fun.

14

Whether on horseback or by your own feet,
Here's a great excuse to get on the beach,
Take in the joys of nature and explore,
Turn your phone off and relax on the shore.

Downtown/LaVilla/The Railyards

Walk/Drive

Due to the industrial nature of this neighborhood, please keep safety your priority.

Downtown Jacksonville is the heart of Jacksonville's business operations. It is not the only place you will find corporate headquarters, but it is the only place you'll find high-rise buildings on the First Coast. Downtown once was a residential hub until the Great Fire of 1901, which started at a mattress factory. Since then, the primary residences of Jacksonville have been spread out in one of the country's most vast urban sprawls. Jacksonville natives have long desired a rejuvenation of its downtown and have slowly seen the addition of flats, townhomes, and apartments. More progress is planned for the future, and with it, many of these celebrated locations will experience a new day in the spotlight.

1

Replacing the first lost by the Great Fire,
You'll recognize this icon by its spire.
Do admire its Gothic Revival face;
The vulnerable of Jax, it's given grace.

2

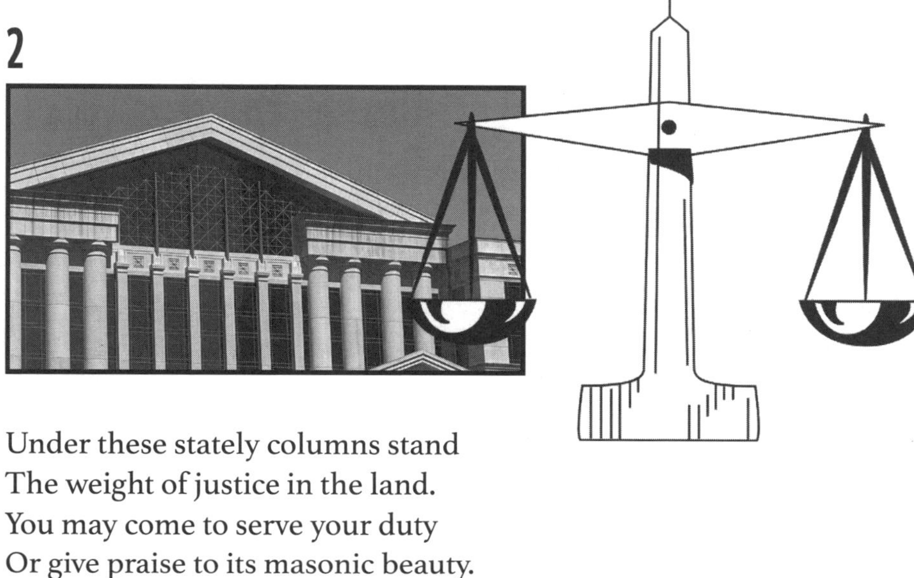

Under these stately columns stand
The weight of justice in the land.
You may come to serve your duty
Or give praise to its masonic beauty.

3

Observe Jax in repeated reflection
When you discover this intersection
At the corner of theatre and art
On this downtown trail you have come to chart.

4

Voted seventh leader of our nation,
Ascending through his varied stations:
Lawyer, statesman, a few of his titles,
His place in our history was vital.

5

If the city you want to see,
The place to begin this must be.
Ask the experts and plan your stay
If you need help along the way.

6

Wandering through the ideas of our time,
Up the colorful five floors you may climb.
Discover static and dynamic sites,
Elevating your consciousness to new heights.

7

I'm gonna let it shine, this light of mine,
Is it a symbol or is it a sign?
Guiding lost souls through desperate waters,
Greeting fathers, mothers, sons, and daughters.

Built on the site of a former prison,
A palace of dreams has since arisen,
A 1920s structure of romance,
In the past, on the rooftop you could dance.

Three halls on the St. Johns for art,
For performances here is where you'll start,
The strings, horns, cymbals, drums, and flutes
Will surely have you tapping your boots.

10

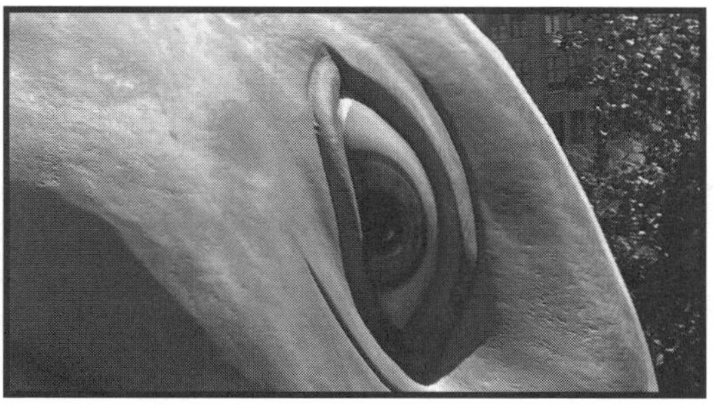

Three names and almost two centuries past,
The oldest park in Jax was meant to last.
Indeed, a controversial history:
What the future holds is a mystery.

11

Once for entry by gentlemen only,
In later years the building sat lonely,
Until a new keeper took a section
And showered the structure in confection.

12

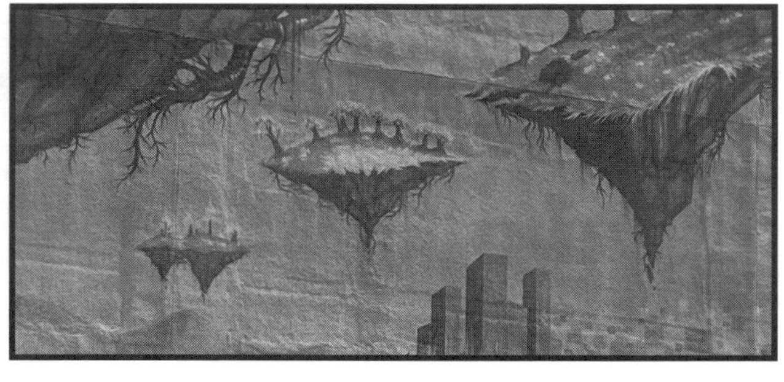

A treasure trove full of discovery,
A hunt from which you might need recovery,
In which case grab a coffee or a snack,
You'll have so much fun, you'll surely be back.

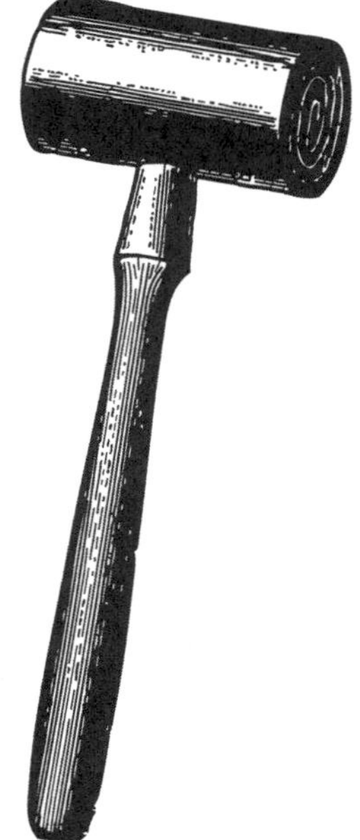

13

The second city structure of its name,
The first burnt down, an historic shame,
Now it's a home for our council to meet,
A place where legislation holds its seat.

14

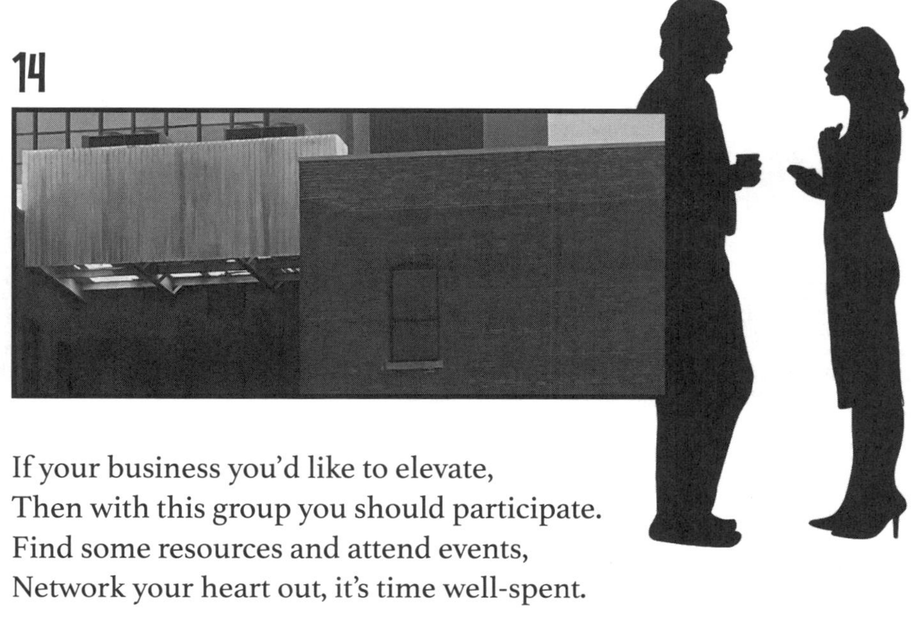

If your business you'd like to elevate,
Then with this group you should participate.
Find some resources and attend events,
Network your heart out, it's time well-spent.

15

Born out of the ashes of the Great Fire,
This historic building's structure was dire,
'Til the present day, when it was restored
And a fine dining chef it has scored.

Imagination come to life
At the tip of a sculpting knife,
Artificial life at its best,
You might laugh, or scream, on this quest.

____

____

17

It's the perfect place to study,
Find a seat and grab a buddy.
You must be quiet, don't forget,
Or unfriendly stares you'll get.

____

____

18

In the Harlem of the South, you can learn
The history of a people who did yearn
For freedom and a voice in a dark past,
Whose story in the Bold City is vast.

____

____

19

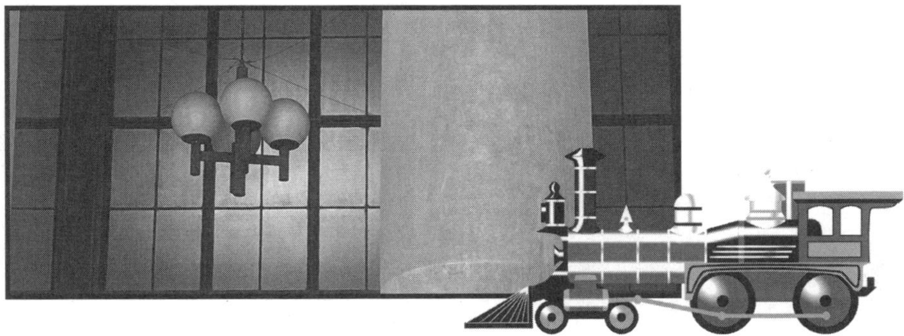

Today it stands as a place to gather;
In the past you would have used it, rather,
As normal means for your commutation,
A now-dated form of transportation.

____

____

20

The city's public transit hub,
It's a party, come and join the club,
Skyway ferry, bus, or rideshare,
You have options to get you there.

21

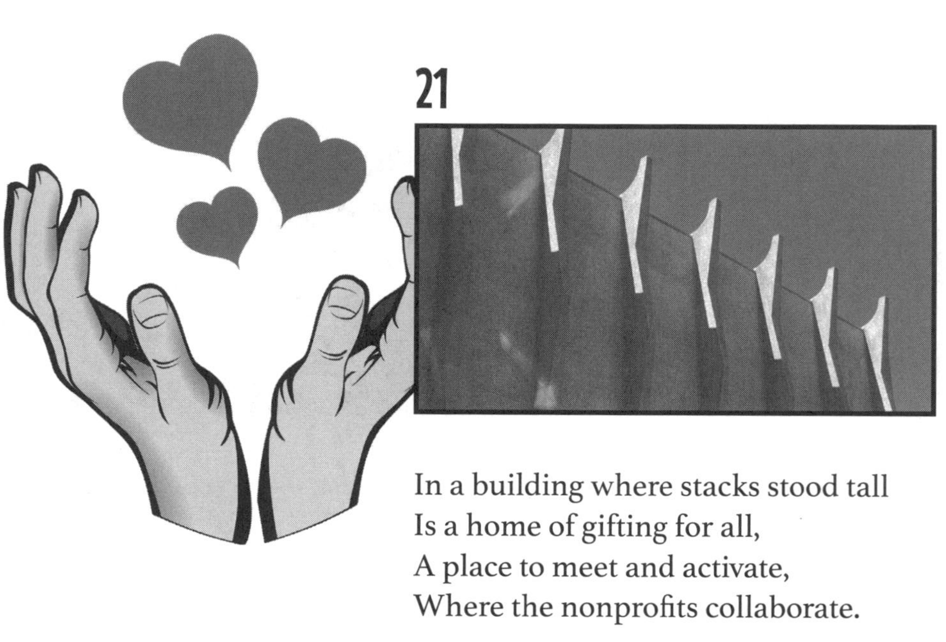

In a building where stacks stood tall
Is a home of gifting for all,
A place to meet and activate,
Where the nonprofits collaborate.

22

Famed as Florida's oldest of its kind,
When on the hunt for produce, you'll find
An array of harvest locally grown:
Over a million guests each year it's known.

____

____

23

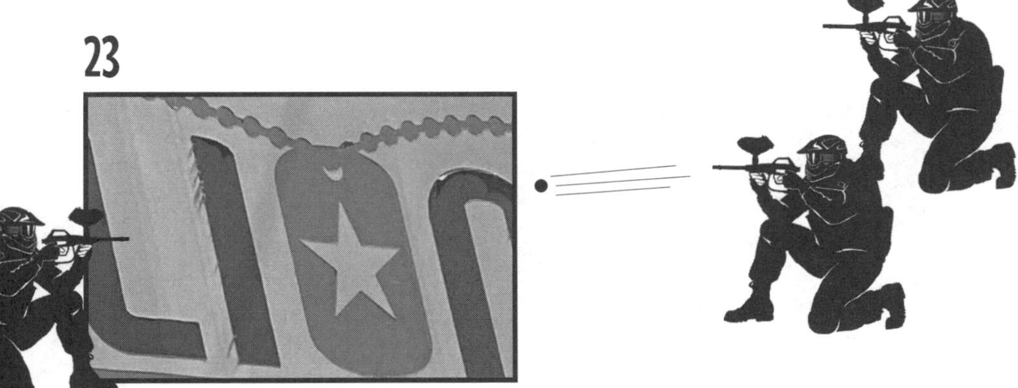

On this mission you can get tactical;
At this arena, it is practical.
In this indoor battlefield, you'll role-play,
Have the time of your life? Yes, you just may.

____

____

24

Quartered in a former book bindery,
Paper isn't its only history.
Their Hispanic lineage empowers,
Whether it's pilsner, lager, stout, or sours.

25

When it's antiques you're hunting for,
There are few places where you'll find more
For remodeling or for decor.
Sifting through here is not a chore.

26

Everyone deserves a clean slate:
This concept is their strongest trait.
Enjoy the green space and a drink,
Gather with friends and watch the sun sink.

27

Whether it's a wedding or makers mart,
This industrial setting is so smart,
Add a little magic and fairy dust
To transport your guests past all of the rust.

Downtown Sports District and Shipyards

Walk

Due to the industrial nature of this neighborhood, please keep safety your priority.

The Sports District is home to the majority of Jacksonville's larger sporting events. It's also your destination for great concerts, comedy, and more. Not only does it host our large arena and football field, it's also a hub for historical treasures, cultural gems, and green space, right on the river. Enjoy a walk around this exciting hub that continues to improve each year.

1

Ice, basketball, and football play here,
So grab some popcorn, and give them a cheer,
Prefer a concert, or maybe some cirque?
Collect your ticket and purchase some merch.

2

When you are feeling on the prowl,
Wear your suit, and bring your towel,
Watch the biggest screens here in Jax,
Level up your day to the max.

3

Once a landfill, now a venue,
Blues were yearly on the menu,
Kids played around the firehouse,
The perfect date for you and your spouse.

4

Outside the arena, you'll find this wall
With the names of officers who did fall.
In the line of their virtuous duty,
They did pay the ultimate price, truly.

5

Savor a brew made by local crafters
In a comfy seat, above the rafters,
While you drink in a panoramic view
Of the Sports District, with your trusted crew.

6

The only church to survive the Great Fire
With its brick masonry, and soaring spire,
Today, you can host a lovely event,
If to the society you pay rent.

7

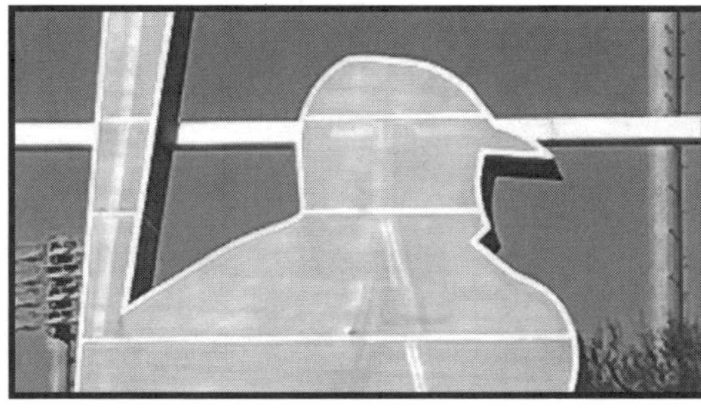

Enjoy some good, old-fashioned fun,
Whether it's a strike, or a home run,
This park's one of the leagues premier,
So grab a snack and give a cheer.

8

Happen by and you might get a whiff
Of a morning drink you like to drip,
It's so delectable, you'll have to stop
And praise how good it is, 'til the last drop.

____

____

9

Available media is vital,
Talking the arts and things political,
This station's been at work 50-plus years,
For all who offer up their eyes and ears.

____

____

10

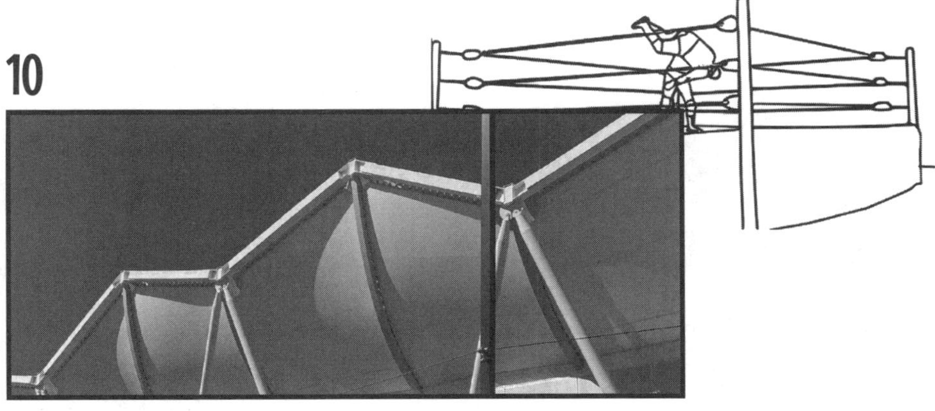

Every town needs an open-air venue,
Let off some steam, and take in the menu,
Any of the acts could make your day,
From music to wrestling, they all come to play.

11

For local info and beyond,
From the field and the parking lot,
Just look across the little pond,
They cover what to do and not.

12

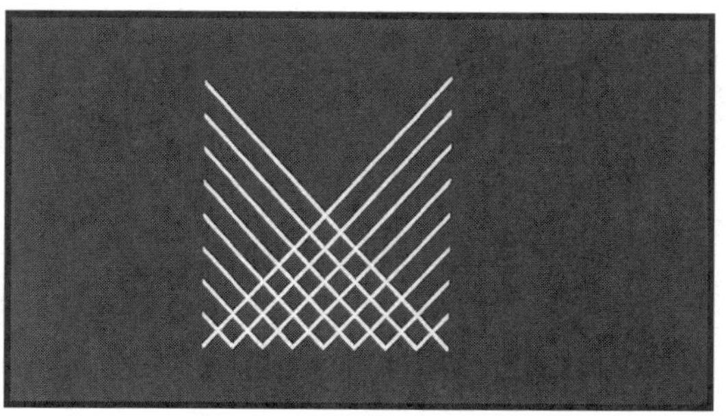

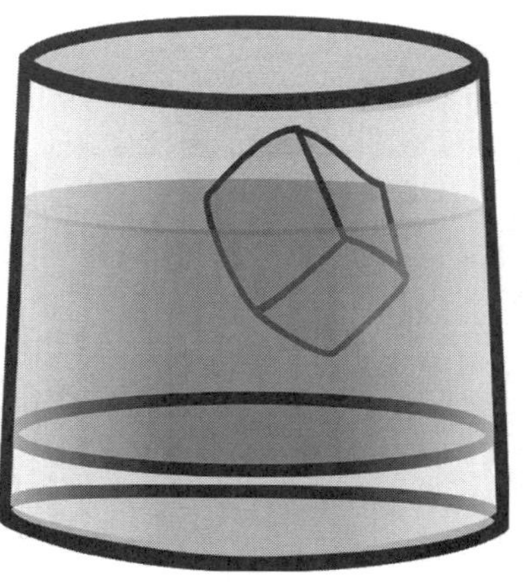

What is in the bottle comes from the heart:
That's the age-old way crafters tend to start,
Organic on a scale that is full-grown,
Just getting started, their name will be known.

13

They are the stewards of Jacksonville's past,
Documenting stories they hope will last,
Keeping this treasure for generations,
Joining the guardians in the nation.

14

A creative space featuring pizza,
For your body and soul it will treat ya,
Markets, music, skaters, and pickleball,
A vibrant collection of faves for all.

15

Your ideal watering hole on game day,
Stay for a while, listen to music play,
Very close to where you need to be,
Whether a baller or diva you'd see.

16

One of nine that span the river,
As you cross it, you might shiver,
Named for the founder of this town,
Eyes ahead, don't dare look down.

17

Relocated not once but now three times,
In the 1900s, the house was nice,
Witness the evolution of fighters
Who withstood the heat when it got tighter.

18

Standing by the eternal flame
Is a reminder of their names,
Representing all of the six factions
Of long-lost heroes who all took action.

Springfield

Walk

Due to the industrial nature of this neighborhood, please keep safety your priority.

Springfield owns the title of Jacksonville's oldest neighborhood. Thanks to the efforts of creative homeowners, it's been undergoing a stunning transformation in the last few years. The bungalows and mansions that Springfield has been known for since the 1800s are being restored to their original splendor, and small business owners are bringing new development to the area. As you search, you're sure to find plenty to explore, especially if you're a history lover!

1

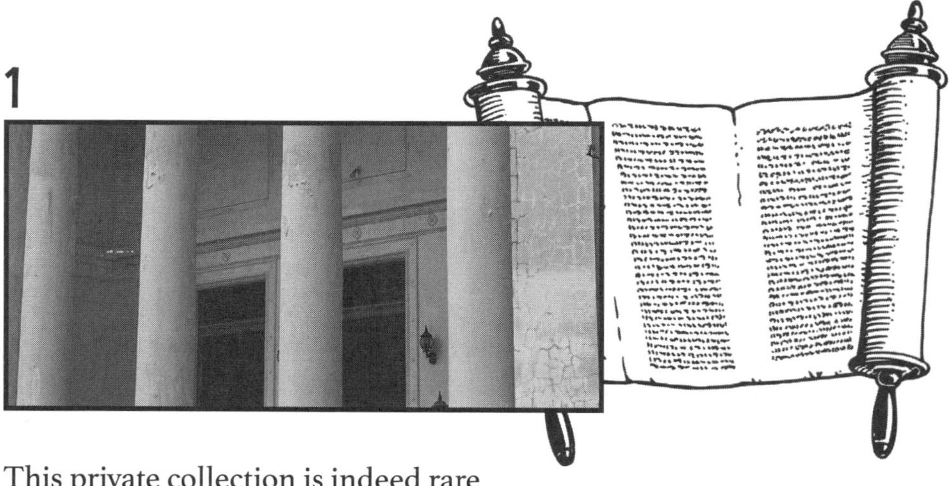

This private collection is indeed rare
In this former house of prayer.
Some of the most brilliant minds
Created the treasures you will find.

2

A hidden treasure locked in time,
Once the home of a splendid mind
Who remade Jax after the Fire
And drafted designs that still inspire.

3

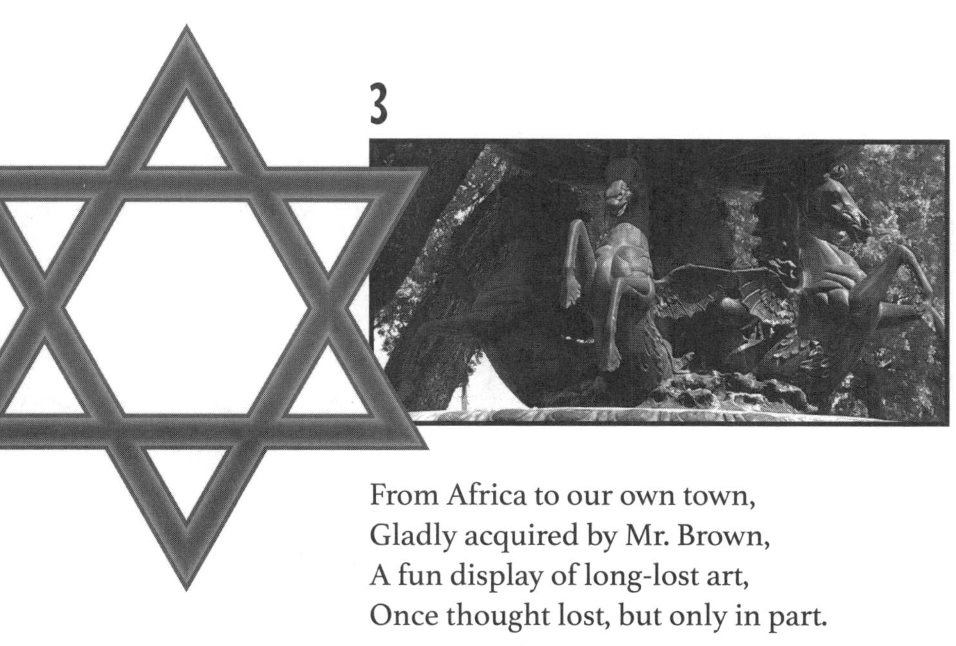

From Africa to our own town,
Gladly acquired by Mr. Brown,
A fun display of long-lost art,
Once thought lost, but only in part.

Designed as a Venetian promenade
And a lovely gazebo by the glade,
One of our city's historic places,
Full of timeless charm and social graces.

5

Over a century it has stood tall,
An iconic structure and meeting hall,
A shrine with an Egyptian theme;
In the 1920s it was a dream.

6

A historic green space with a new name,
A new chapter, but lovely, just the same,
To controversy it is no stranger:
Sometimes, before change, there must come anger.

____

____

7

It's historic, but not the oldest,
In our city of some of the boldest,
A notable resting place aged through time,
Some famous memorials you may find.

____

____

8

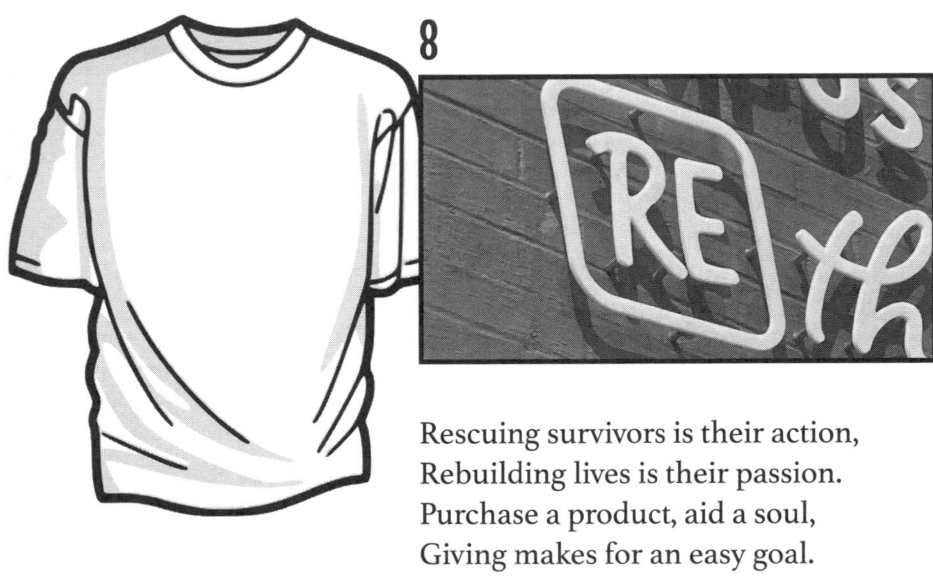

Rescuing survivors is their action,
Rebuilding lives is their passion.
Purchase a product, aid a soul,
Giving makes for an easy goal.

9

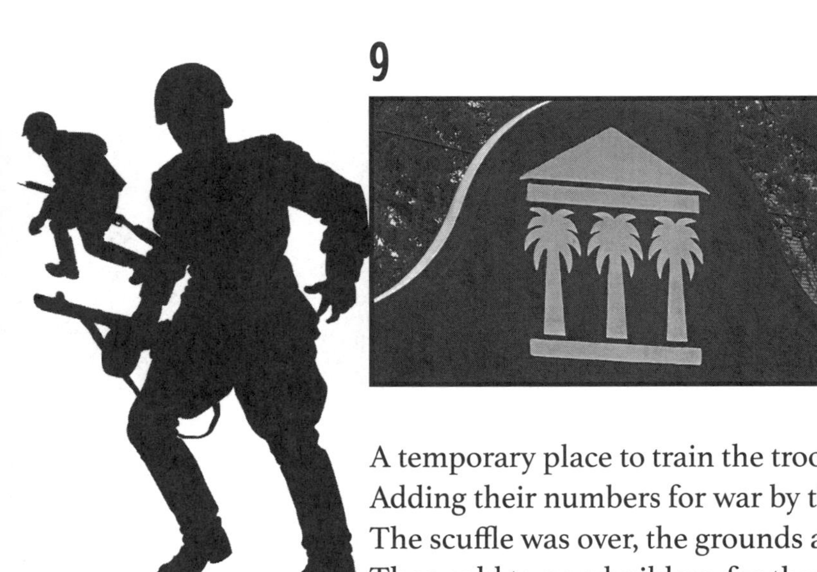

A temporary place to train the troops,
Adding their numbers for war by the groups,
The scuffle was over, the grounds alone,
Then sold to new builders, for them to own.

10

They come to learn and come to heal;
The trauma cases here are real,
Not for the faint of heart to see,
If a doctor or nurse you'll be.

Southbank

Walk

This small parcel of land sits on the river and is framed by the San Marco neighborhood. Highlighted by sweeping views of downtown Jacksonville, Southbank's stunning skyrise condos have attracted city dwellers who have made them their home. Adjacent to these luxury flats is the sprawling medical complex of Baptist Health and Wolfson Children's Hospital. Take a water taxi or walk across the John T. Alsop Bridge for easy access to the urban core.

1

Walk, jog, or take in the city skyline,
Perfect place to sit and pass the time,
A mile and a quarter on the water:
Soon, you'll be an expert dolphin spotter.

2

What began for children is now for all,
History, planets, and creatures enthrall,
Become a member and enjoy the perks
Brought by generous donations and works.

3

Once the biggest and tallest of its kind,
Finished with camaraderie on the mind,
Over 17,000 gallons spray,
So tempting, but you can't get in and play.

4

Perhaps the oldest living thing in Jax,
Never to be taken to with an ax.
The city's most charitable did toil
To keep it rooted firmly in the soil.

5

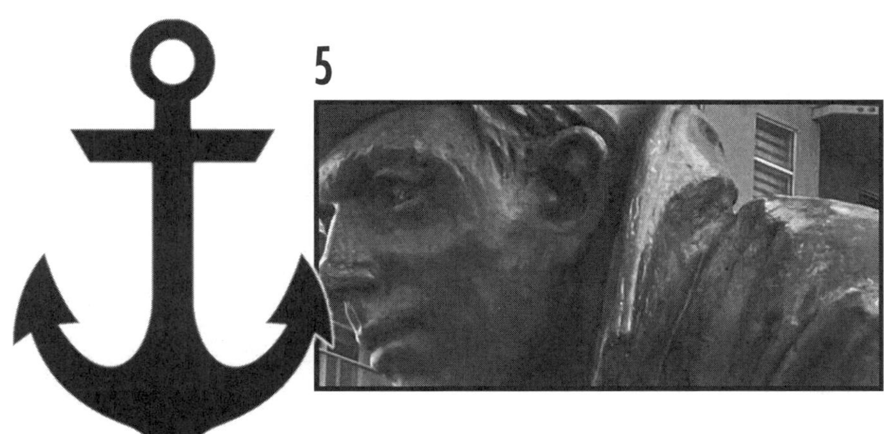

He stands looking out over the St. Johns,
No brothers around him; they are all gone,
A part of the city that makes us stout,
An example of what Jax is all about.

6

If help for a young one you do seek,
Your time here will be great, not bleak,
Caring for offspring is their charge,
And in the region they are large.

____

____

7

One of the most visible of all nine,
Make sure if you cross to give it some time,
You never know when up it will lift:
Its image on the skyline is a gift.

____

____

8

Hop on here for some free transportation,
Get an aerial tour from this station,
A quick way to cross over the river,
Don't look down, or you might give a shiver.

9

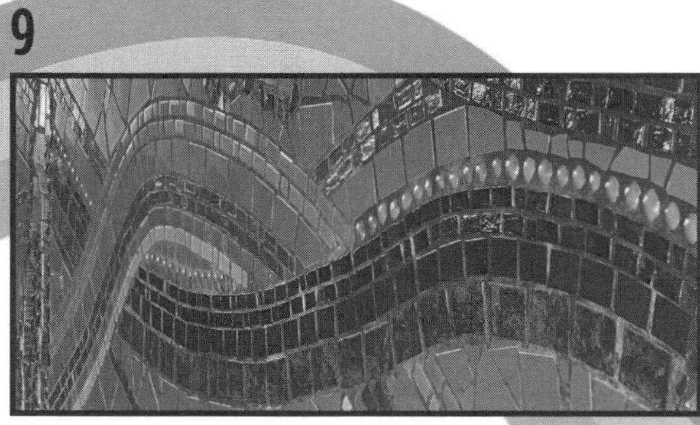

The river floats northward, just like the Nile;
Now it's public art, made of mirrored tile,
Can you find your reflection? Where are you?
You will find this hidden, under Big Blue.

10

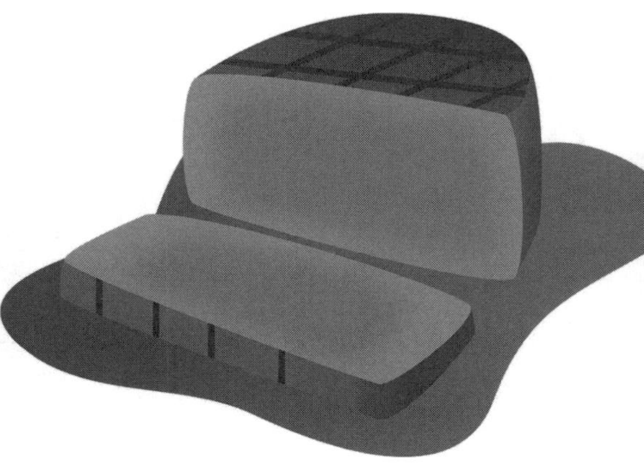

An iconic place to dine in,
A shell-shaped building, have you been?
Order the lobster or the steak,
Or try a cocktail, for a break.

Riverside

Walk

Riverside is one of the most historic and culturally diverse neighborhoods in Jacksonville. A hub for art and a dining destination, Riverside offers plenty of opportunities for exploration. Attend a farmers market, meander through a museum, or visit a local brewery. There's something for everyone in this community by the river.

1

The second-oldest park in the city,
Its spring-fed lake and fount are so pretty,
Perfect for yoga under shade trees,
Enjoy the dog park and take in the breeze.

2

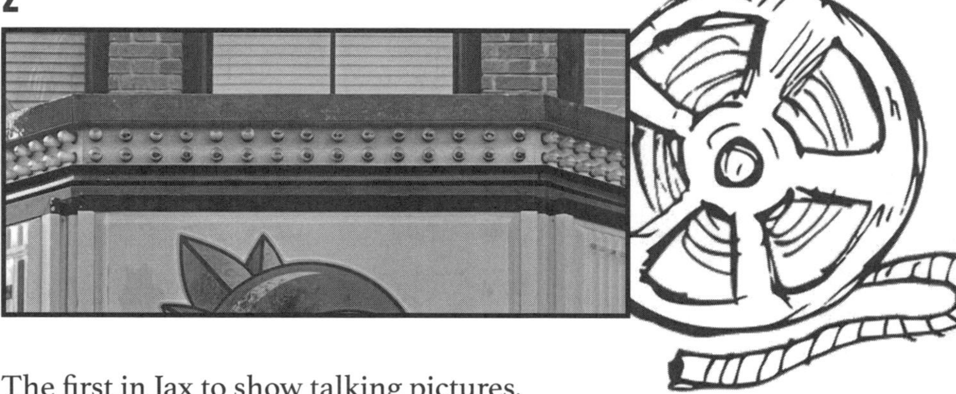

The first in Jax to show talking pictures,
Now a well-known, indie film fixture,
Purchase a ticket for one of two screens,
A blockbuster, or bio, if you're keen.

3

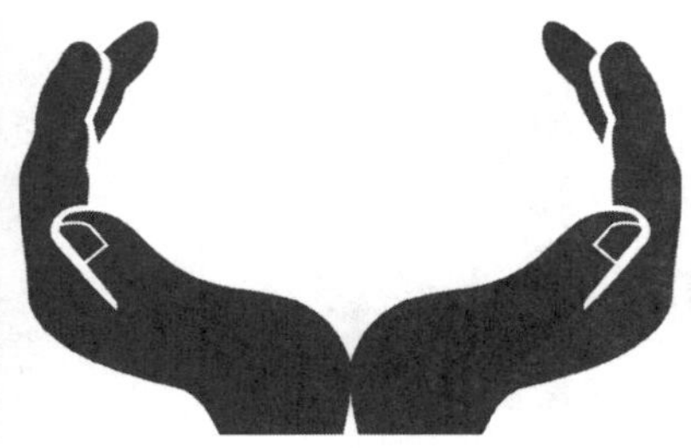

Birthed from an experience in a tent,
Who knew what this revival really meant?
Now a long, compassionate gathering,
Embracing the community under their wing.

4

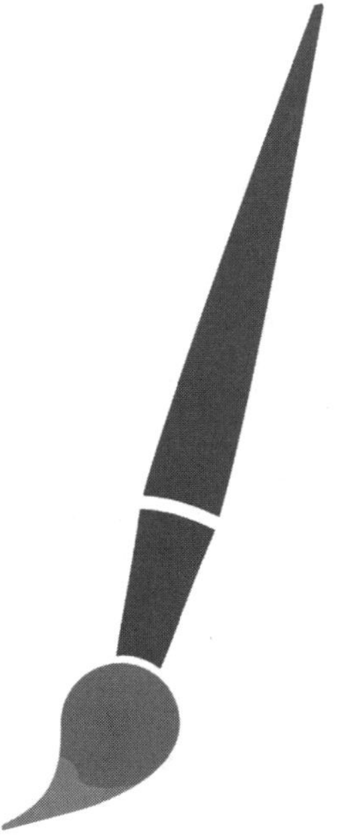

If it's the therapy of art you crave,
Then over the exhibitions you'll rave,
Meander the gardens, all three pretty,
While you drink in the views of the city.

5

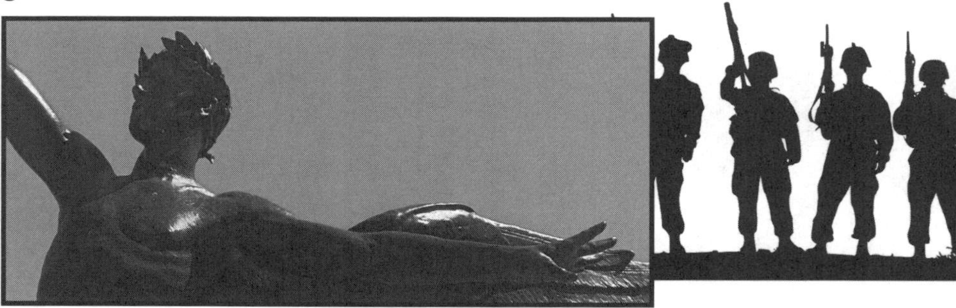

Remembering those lost in World War I,
Go here to relax or take in the sun,
The third-oldest park in this huge city,
The figure on the globe is so pretty.

6

At the pentacle of these lanes,
Experiences you will gain,
Shopping, dining, and timeless art
Are found right here, along the path's heart.

7

With the group goal to enhance the city,
This institution made Jax so pretty,
Saving oak trees, and planting many new,
Reimagining parks, their passion grew.

8

Mediterranean Revival style,
This '30s structure has been here a while,
Quiet and sweet, it's the perfect retreat
To stack up the books, for a study meet.

9

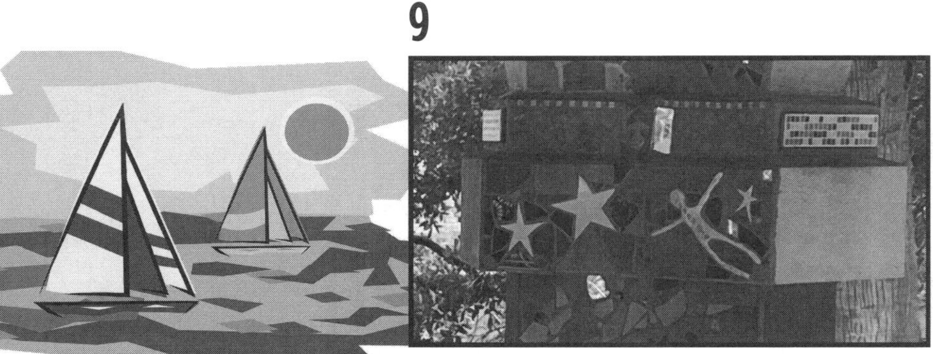

This quiet retreat is peaceful and warm,
Look for the lovely mosaic which forms
A stunning aesthetic in the arbor,
Standing watch over waterfront harbor.

10

In 1916, The Daughters did found
A place for treatment and care centered 'round
The Catholic beliefs that they held true,
Serving the sick, whether many or few.

11

Its clever name is a mixture
Of the streets it is a fixture,
Support the tenant creatives:
Purchase local from our natives.

This local home became the place
Where a now-famous band made space
To jam out and one day create
Classic rock we all celebrate.

13

Cocktails at sunset with a birds-eye view,
Gather with friends and play games with a few,
Mingle with singles or take up some pool,
No question: this watering hole is so cool.

14

Make sure to order the dusty boot,
It's casual here, you don't need a suit,
The ideal place to dine under the sky,
From patio to rooftop with your guy.

15

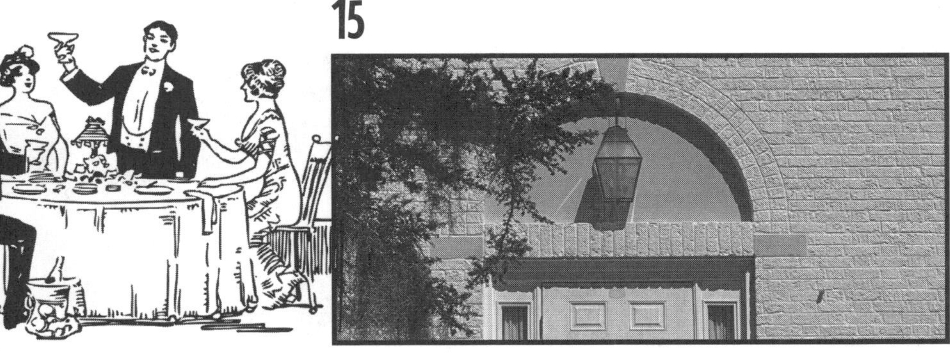

From house of worship to Junior League space,
Weddings to birthdays, these events have grace.
This place was built in the roaring '20s;
About this venue, you will rave plenty.

Murray Hill

Walk/Drive

Murray Hill may be one of Jacksonville's older neighborhoods, but it's not lost in the past. Recently, Murray Hill has been evolving, as young professional families have moved in and called it their own. Creative energy can be felt radiating through local art, delicious dining, and unique small businesses. It seems like only the beginning of what will be a total reimagining of this historic and eclectic neighborhood.

1

Built in the '30s for the silver screen,
But in the '90s it became a scene,
A place for positive nightlife and dance,
Giving wholesome acts a place and chance.

2

Sitting across from a very old school
Is a quaint green space that is a jewel.
Climb and play or toss a ball with a friend;
It's truly a classic, above all trends.

____

____

3

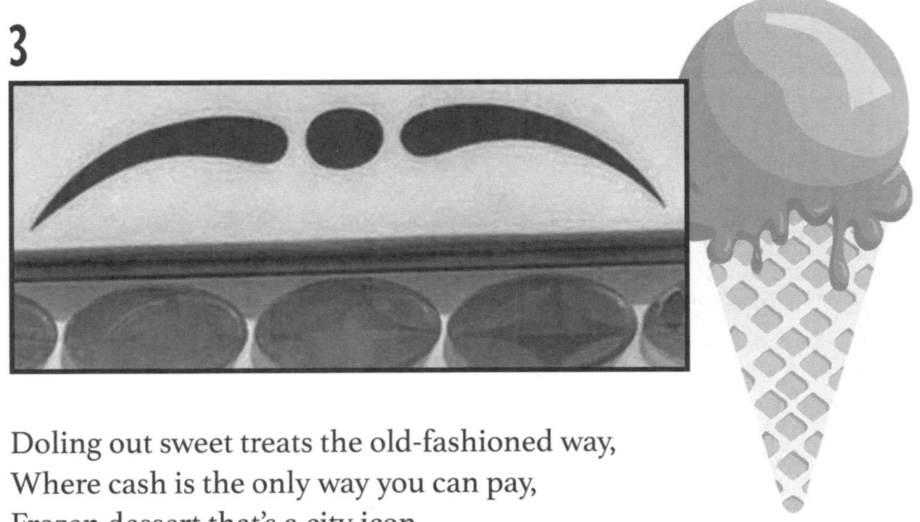

Doling out sweet treats the old-fashioned way,
Where cash is the only way you can pay,
Frozen dessert that's a city icon,
Good service and products keep the lights on.

____

____

A pleasant space to take an active jog
Or have a relaxing walk with your dog,
Meet at Lawnview and Lamboll for some fun.
After playing, perhaps a treat when you're done?

5

It doesn't get hotter than this,
Fresh-baked bread might just be pure bliss,
Grab a coffee and order brunch,
With your friends you will love to munch.

6

Timeless treasures await you in this shop,
And many stories you are sure to swap,
Music, plants, fun events, and local art,
Shopping unique gifts here is smart.

7

A beloved local chef brings us some spice,
It's straight from Texas and it tastes so nice!
Such authentic and flavorful dishes,
And gluten-free, if those are your wishes.

8

If you need to study or to unwind,
Then come to visit, and expand your mind.
Knowledge awaits here for you to borrow:
Visit today, don't wait for tomorrow.

____

____

9

Expand your skills in creativity,
Take a class full of positivity.
You can sculpt, paint, draw, and mold,
Explore your inspiration and be bold.

____

____

10

Local honey is truly a treasure,
The benefits are well beyond measure,
This small town spot cultivates many hives,
Creating something sweet while enhancing lives.

Avondale

Walk

Historic Avondale lies on the borders of Riverside, and often they are paired together. Impressive riverfront mansions, architectural gems, and historic treasures will be found along your journey through this charming and well-preserved neighborhood.

1

If you'd like some boutique shopping,
Then maybe give a thought to stopping,
You can shop, walk around, and dine,
The perfect day: it is so fine.

2

A stunning sight the stained glass makes,
One and all, it opens and takes,
Unconditional love they give,
Serving equally all who live.

3

This park is almost a century old,
Found here in the great city of the Bold,
Bought from a locomotive repairman,
Now you can run, play, or lay out and tan.

4

World-class cocktails and French Southern dining,
Upscale fare that keeps Jacksonville shining,
A night here makes for the ultimate date,
Trendy and casual fare that's top-rate.

____

____

5

Learn from the past or doomed to repeat it
Reason alone to sit for a wee bit
To listen and learn 'bout tales of the past
The South rife with stories, history vast.

____

____

6

A favorite spot for ladies who lunch,
Or perhaps you're more in the mood for brunch?
Whatever you're craving, it's here you'll meet,
Especially if you'd like something sweet.

____

____

7

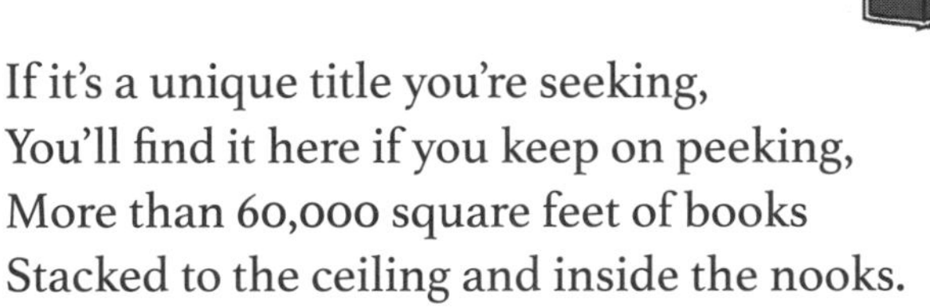

If it's a unique title you're seeking,
You'll find it here if you keep on peeking,
More than 60,000 square feet of books
Stacked to the ceiling and inside the nooks.

____

____

Westside

Drive

The Westside of Jacksonville is perhaps one of the largest areas to explore. Rural farmland, nature preserves, and a host of sporting facilities have ample room to take up the space they need to operate at their best. You'll have to keep your engines turning for this search, as you'll be driving miles between many of the destinations.

1

When racing moto, they're Florida's best,
The athletes who compete here sweep the rest,
Give your bike some gas and catch some more air,
At this ranch you'll soar higher, if you dare.

2

Three trails in one, this former railroad
Is now a path with a different code,
Horseback, biking, jogging, walk, or inline
Through a historic park, under the pines.

3

Take an adventure back in time,
A lovely hike when weather's fine,
Witness replicas from the War,
Explore the trails; you'll surely want more.

4

Here, you will find a hidden waterfall,
A natural treasure preserved for all,
Known as the Cracker Swamp in days of auld,
Now, by its bovine alias it's called.

____

____

5

In this semi-outdoor exchange,
You might have to ask for some change,
Shopping here is only with cash
When replenishing your stash.

____

____

6

The final resting place of Ron Van Zant,
Peace and serenity it surely grants
To all of those who have gone on before,
The ancestors within, and those in store.

7

Built for pilot training in World War II,
Now for public operation it's used,
Gliders, some blimps, and fearless skydiving,
Love aviation sports? Here, it's thriving.

8

If you have a buggy or kart,
You'll think this city park is smart,
Practice rounds on the asphalt track,
It's so much fun, you'll clearly be back.

9

If you have prime, you won't be blue
Arriving in one day or two
Delivered by folks working hard,
Driving your order to your yard.

10

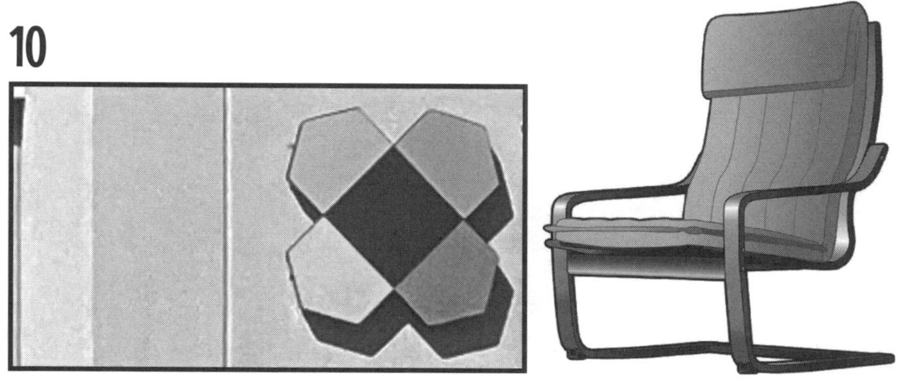

If it's home decor, and you want more,
Then you've probably already shopped at this store,
From online to your home it goes,
Sent with haste, the order you chose.

____

____

11

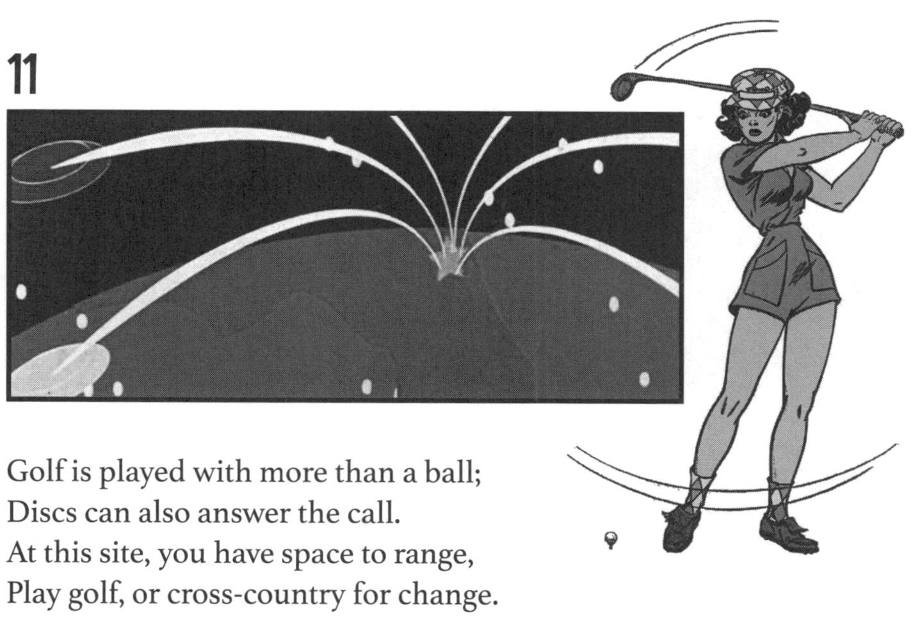

Golf is played with more than a ball;
Discs can also answer the call.
At this site, you have space to range,
Play golf, or cross-country for change.

____

____

12

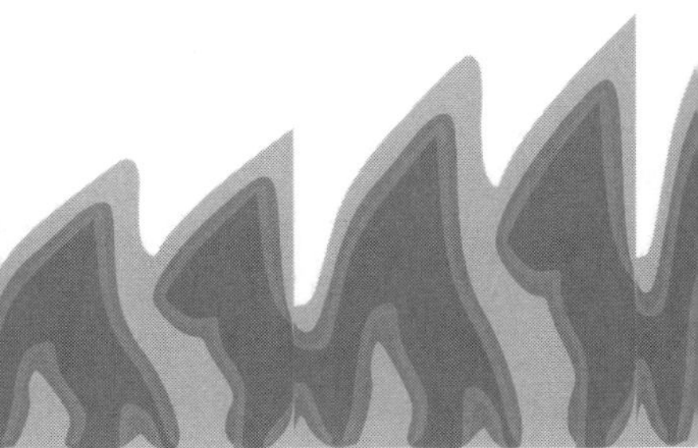

In this wide-open 'hood there still lurks threat,
But these brave heroes aren't afraid to sweat,
They'll go the extra mile, high or low,
And rescue those in danger, fast or slow.

____

____

13

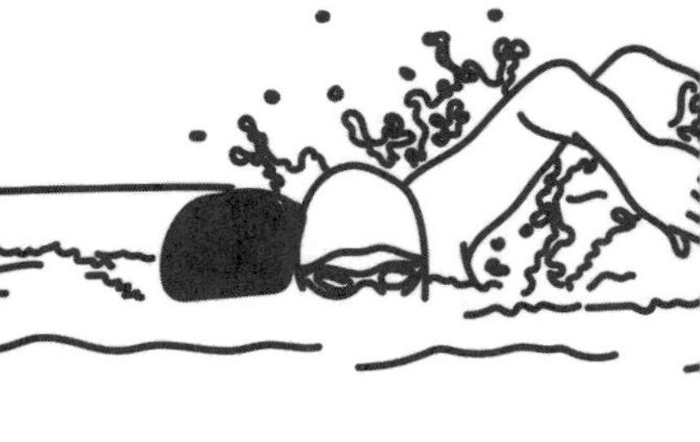

For recreation or for fun,
Completely covered, there's no sun,
Come on in, the water is fine,
Open daily, just find the time.

____

____

14

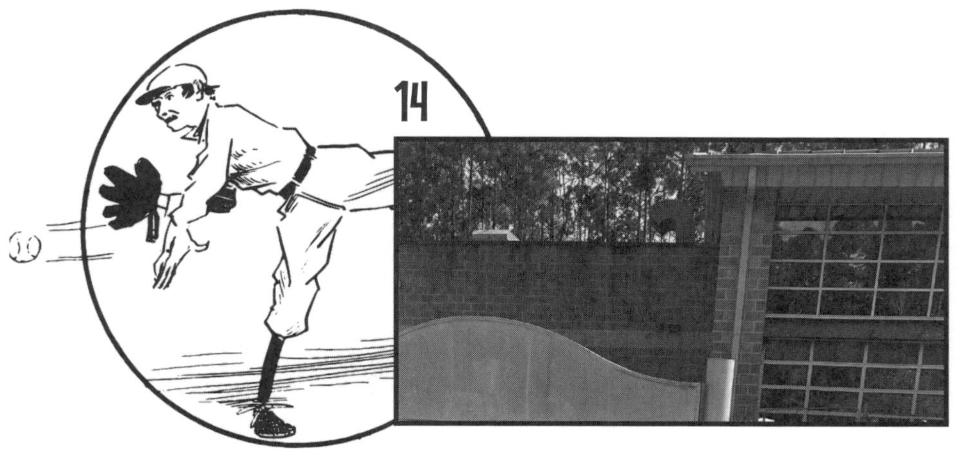

Wind it up and let it gain speed,
Practice is how you plant the seed,
Success before the game is done,
When you achieve your best home run.

15

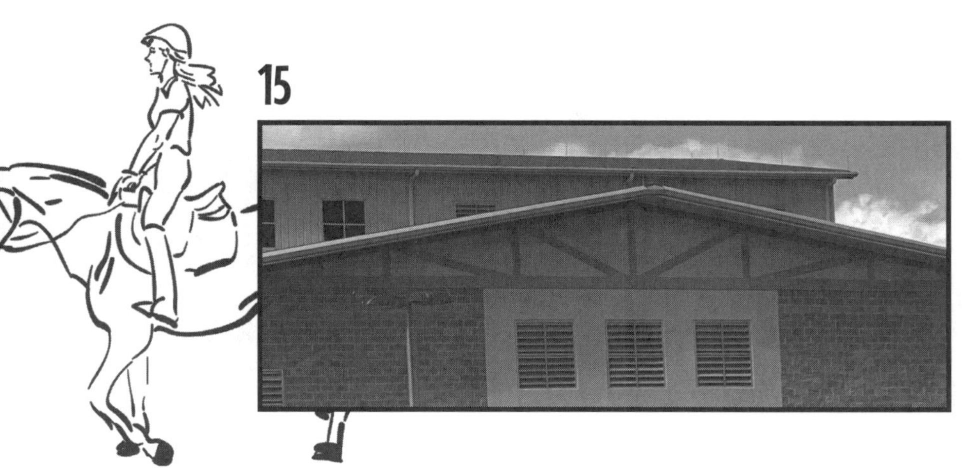

Against your rival you are hot to trot
When you leave with the ribbon you came and sought,
Whether it's dressage or a barrel race,
You'll be leaving with a smile on your face.

A place to worship and to remember
Those lost in action who once were members
Of the military station here past,
Memorializing all of those who've passed.

What now is an industrial center
Once was restricted for you to enter,
The Navy still makes a cameo,
But now it's run by a different show.

18

A peaceful retreat under shady pines,
Your secret escape when the sun does shine,
A picnic, a playground, and fun for all,
And cheer on your team when they play ball.

____

____

19

The perfect place to take your equine friend,
Yes, fresh air and sunshine the heart do mend,
Miles of trails when you kayak, hike, or ride,
Flowers, streams, and forests will be your guide.

____

____

San Marco

Walk/Drive

San Marco is one of Jacksonville's oldest and most treasured neighborhoods. Originally incorporated as its own town, South Jacksonville, the neighborhood's development name, San Marco, became the new alias after the town was eventually annexed into Jacksonville proper. Visitors love admiring the historic riverside mansions, dining at one of the hip foodie destinations, and shopping at trendy boutiques in San Marco Square (inspired by the original in Venice). Your exploration will also get you up-close and personal with the abundance of green space in the area. There is much historical significance here and no lack of good, old-fashioned, Southern American charm.

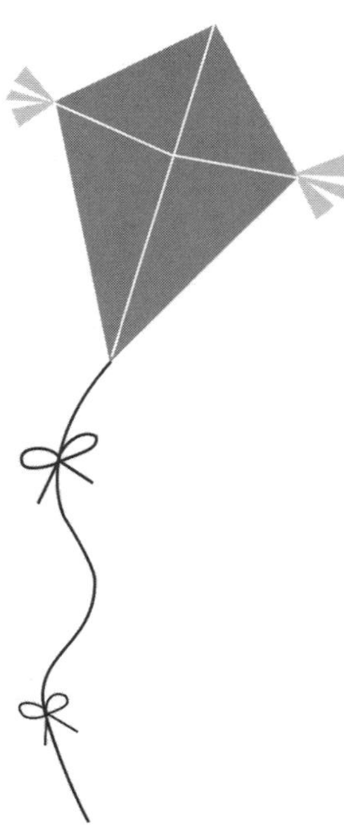

1

See the kids laugh and the dog play,
What to do on a perfect day?
When the weather behaves just right,
Then it's time to fly a kite.

____

____

2

If in San Marco you are in trouble,
They will be there to aid on the double,
There to help if ever you are in need,
Beat the heat, or perhaps lend you some speed.

3

Where once a service station stood
Now sits a rotunda made of wood
In the midst of the center square
Near a reflecting pool so fair.

4

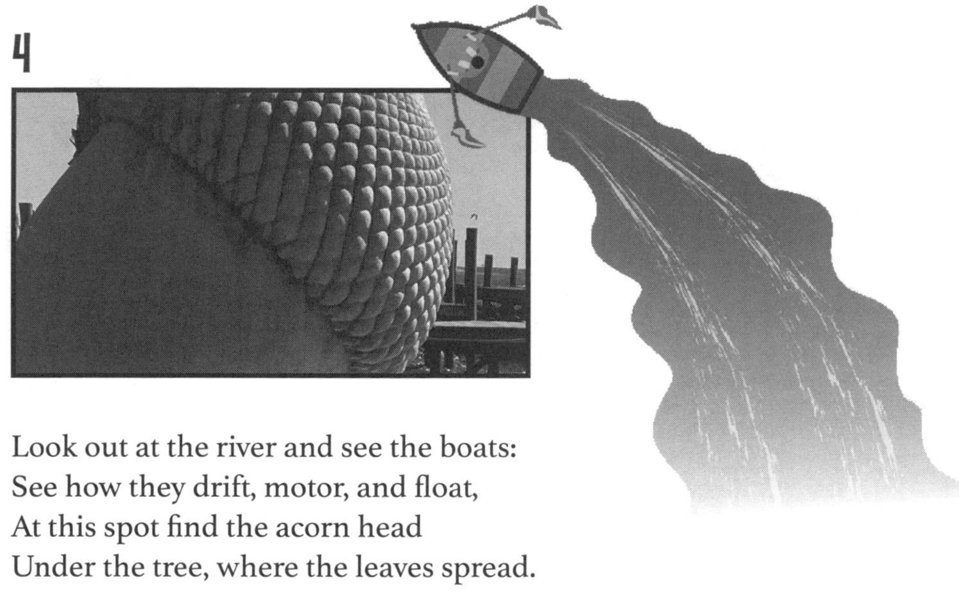

Look out at the river and see the boats:
See how they drift, motor, and float,
At this spot find the acorn head
Under the tree, where the leaves spread.

5

San Marco's symbol is noble and bold,
Here, like in Venice, their story is told,
Not one but three looking out from their stream,
Beholding their charge, as if in a dream.

6

The same designer as two others here,
Entertaining patrons since yesteryear,
Arthouse flicks kept it alive in downtimes,
Now, two silver screens keep it in its prime.

7

The oldest building in San Marco stands,
Celebrating couples with joining hands,
The ideal event or wedding venue,
Old St. Paul's is still present here with you.

8

Named for one of San Marco's creators
Who also built one of the "the-ay-ters."
Sadly, he passed with his wife in a car,
His memory lives here, and in the stars.

9

Pizza, pasta, cocktails, and cheese,
Your order is very likely to please,
One of San Marco's favorite haunts,
Don't miss this tasty restaurant.

10

Over 100 years of showmanship,
Performing the arts and learning the script,
Christened the city's official playhouse,
It's the perfect date night with your spouse.

11

A gathering place to chat and to dine,
Don't miss the wine list, it's rather fine,
Family owned with a tasty menu,
This intimate space is a great venue.

12

Named for a family in high esteem,
Since the 1800s, they lived the dream.
Today, this park honors their tradition,
While children play on this fun addition.

____

____

13

The city views are the most appealing
From this bulkhead park you may see reeling,
Fishing, strolling, this cozy esplanade,
An evening sunset here you will applaud.

____

____

14

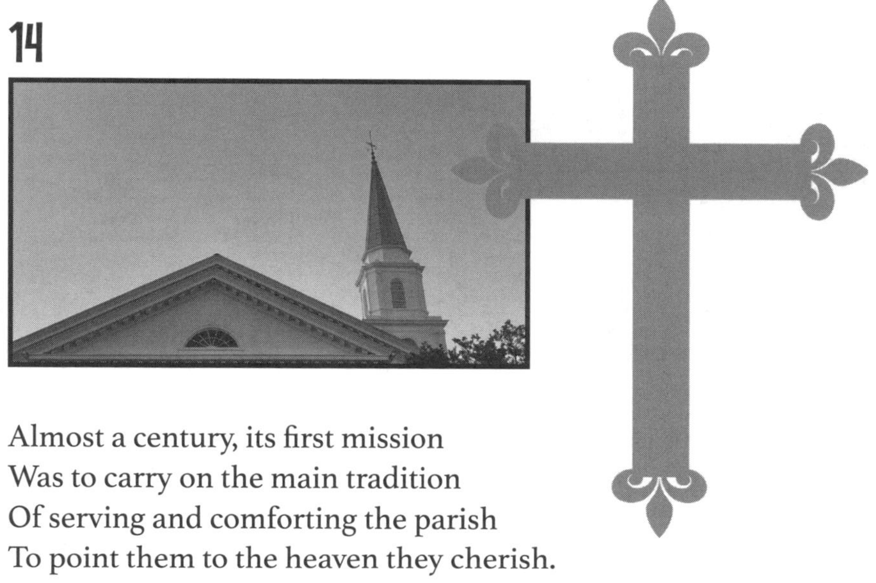

Almost a century, its first mission
Was to carry on the main tradition
Of serving and comforting the parish
To point them to the heaven they cherish.

15

A building once used as an ice warehouse
Has today transformed into an alehouse,
Winning awards for their delicious brews,
The only tough call is which one to choose.

16

Across from this green space once was a school,
Now turned into lofts, it's quite the jewel,
The lawn is now a peaceful getaway
For quiet reflection and children's play.

17

If you're looking for the perfect title,
Then a visit here, you'll find, is vital.
Some things are just better not online,
Like turning a page, or a glass of wine.

18

They call this space a "pocket park,"
It might be small, but still makes its mark,
Situated with a riverfront view,
It's small yet mighty and known by a few.

19

The bricks for local homes used clay
From the pit where this lake does lay,
A secret to most, except few
Who've lived here and history knew.

20

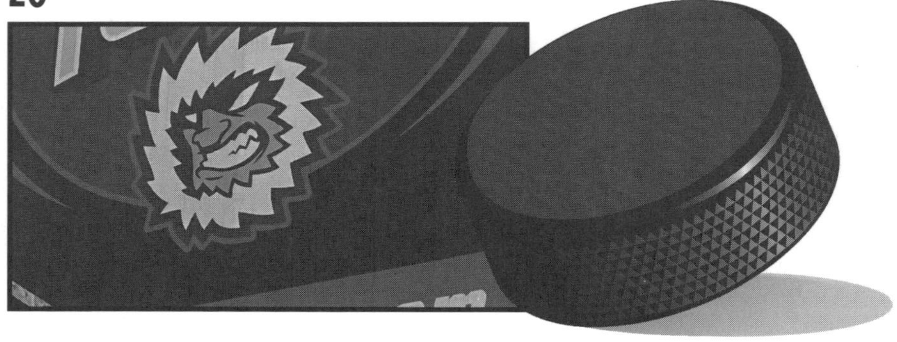

Who says Florida's too hot to find ice?
A day here is fun at a decent price.
Now, its redesign is state of the art,
If you enjoy hockey, here's where to start.

21

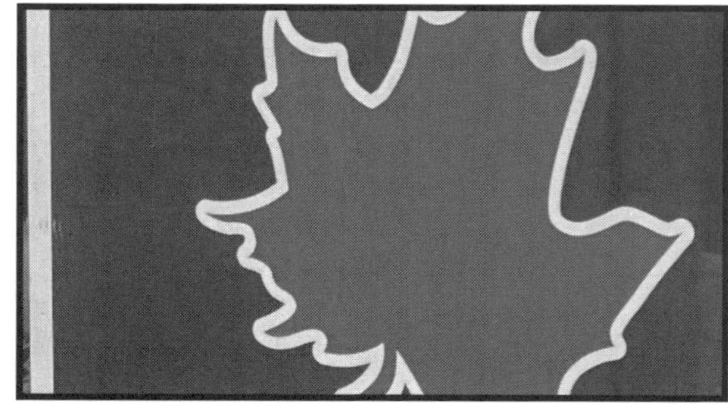

Breakfast has become a lifestyle,
We come for comfort, and a smile,
They are biscuit-making adept,
With a modern secret they have kept.

22

What's more classic? Burgers or pizza pie?
Eaten alone, or served with some french fries?
For decades these experts have served them up,
Also known for the tomato bisque cup.

____

____

23

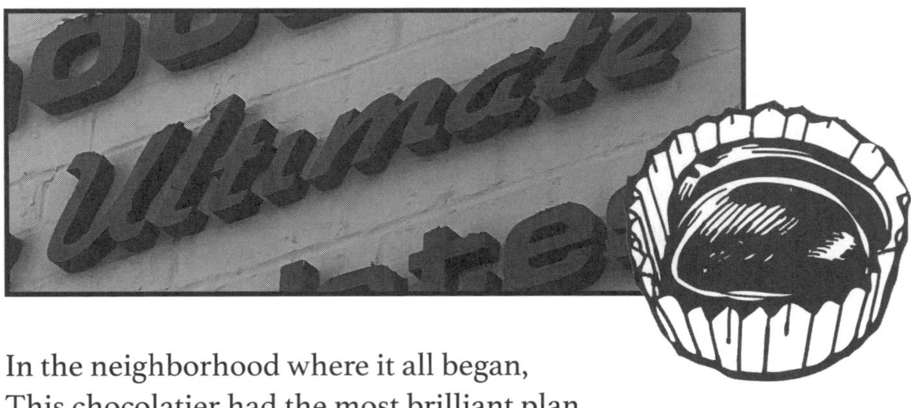

In the neighborhood where it all began,
This chocolatier had the most brilliant plan,
Named after her children, it was a hit,
From popcorn to pretzels, this place is lit.

____

____

24

A San Marco culinary treasure,
Dining here's an ultimate pleasure,
French and Mediterranean cuisine,
On delectable dishes, you'll be keen.

25

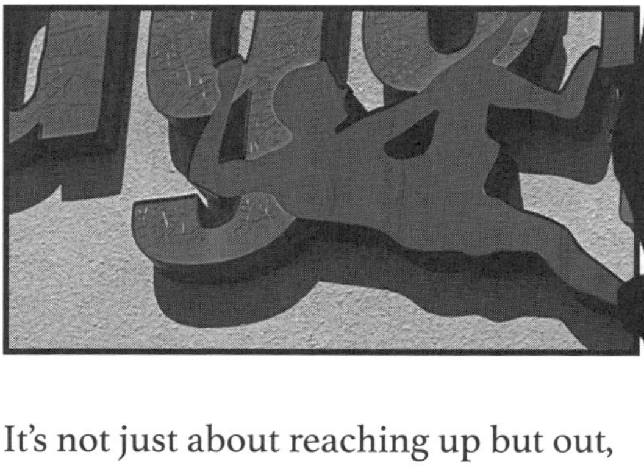

It's not just about reaching up but out,
When you try this, a new passion may sprout,
A place you can get your adventure on,
Invest in yourself, and new strength you'll spawn.

26

This locale is all for the love of food,
The perfect comfort when you're in a mood,
Come experience their first location
In what became a foodie sensation.

Arlington

Drive

Perhaps one of the most underrated neighborhoods in Jacksonville, Arlington is a wide, sprawling space whose main draw is its natural wonders and important role in history. One of the first places in the nation to be visited by Europeans, Arlington, in addition to charming suburban subdivisions, houses the nation's oldest skate park, delightful Southern cuisine, and some of the best biodiversity in the city.

1

One hundred and two acres to inspect,
You'll be in awe of nature, I suspect,
Grab your kayak, fishing pole, and some gear,
This might be your favorite place all year.

2

This 18-hole golf course did evolve
Into a space that keeps nature involved,
Preserving sensitive natural land,
While humans enjoy, and still lend a hand.

3

A private institution with high praise,
If accepted, you'll be thrilled for the days
Where dolphins are cheered on by their classmates,
Inside and out of these hallowed gates.

4

An icon for sweet treats for six decades,
Year after year, they keep making the grade,
Folks line up to grab them, hoard, and stash,
Always make sure to remember your cash!

5

If you're in Lake Lucina on a lark,
Do not miss this intimate pocket park,
Let your tots run around, to chase and play,
While under the shade you enjoy the day.

6

With 50 acres of Florida trails,
Immersed in nature, heal what ails,
Visit the exhibits, including goats,
You'll have plenty of memories to boast.

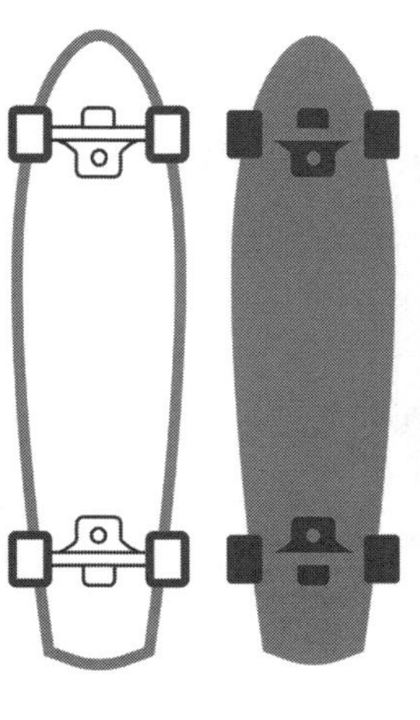

7

The oldest operating park of its kind,
Famous athletes keep it top of mind,
Learn from the pros: this place changed the game,
So many legends from here rose to fame.

8

From strip mine to natural paradise,
Over 100 acres, it's so nice,
Sit by the lake or meander a trail,
Screen time versus time in nature does pale.

9

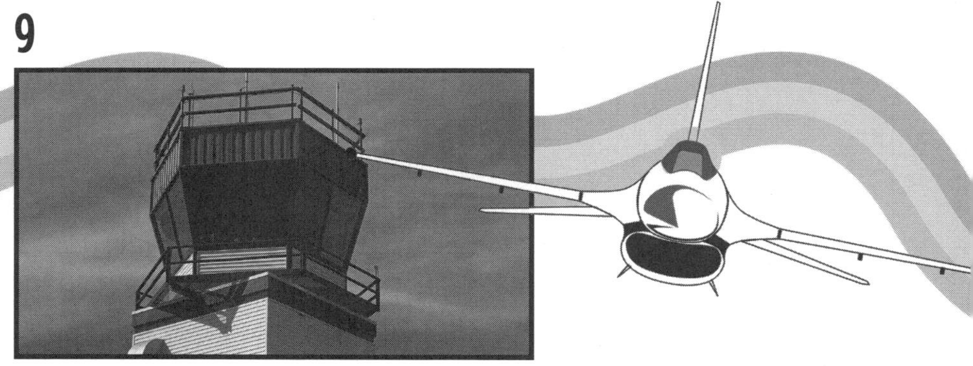

If, when you travel, private you prefer,
They will give you wings and won't cause a stir,
For those still seeking an education,
You have found a place in aviation.

10

This park was named for a former mayor,
You'll love it if you're a disc-golf player,
Over 100 acres of pure fun,
A skate park, trails, and soccer fields to run.

11

The French attempted to settle this site,
Alas, they decidedly lost that fight.
The ancient Timucua people lived here,
Sadly, their history is lost and unclear.

Southside

Drive

Jacksonville's Southside includes a large expanse of both business and residential communities. It's perhaps the most diverse region, and you will move in and out of industrial complexes, historical neighborhoods, and modern-day shopping centers. From the intracoastal waterway to the river, the boundary is wide, so fill up your gas tank and enjoy the drive.

1

How this family started their empire,
Love of food and people was their fire,
From fishing this spot to serving fresh eats,
A staple in dining when friends you meet.

2

Immerse yourself in natural marshland,
Take in the views, panoramic and grand,
Push off on a kayak, or take a trail,
For spotting birds, this is not a fail.

3

Celebrating the passion of the race,
A collection of autos that kept pace,
Privately owned, make your reservation,
Go visit! No need for hesitation.

A place of learning engulfed by the wild,
Get out in nature, the weather is mild,
These trails are surprising, and those who know,
300 acres to run and to go.

____

____

5

The oldest in the nation still running,
If for entertainment you're gunning,
Enjoy dinner and a fantastic show,
With the entire family you can go.

____

____

6

If you are ready to shop 'til you drop,
Then at this well-known center you must stop,
Saunter around in the fresh, open air,
And have a bite of the delicious fare.

7

Purchased from a family ranch,
Today a Southside green space branch,
Pickleball, tennis, and much more,
Play some soccer and keep the score.

8

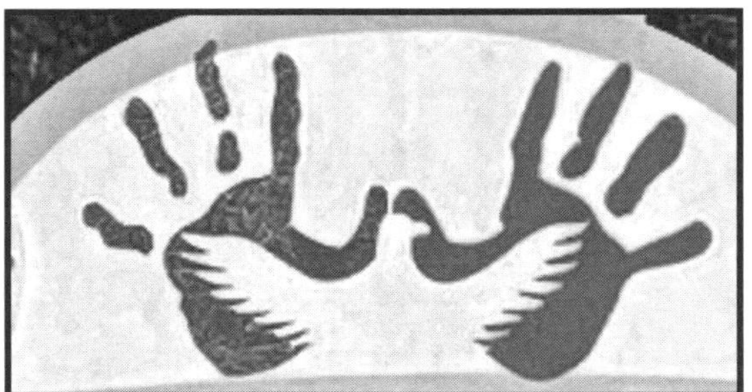

A volunteer effort brought this park heart,
Handicap-accessible and so smart,
It may be small, but it sure has might,
Kids carefree at play, a lovely sight.

___

___

9

When you shop, try not to get lost,
Folks come here for goods at low cost,
Don't forget to try the meatballs,
They're the perfect treat with your haul.

___

___

10

If your floof loves to swim and play,
Then a trip to this park will make their day.
Let the dogs burn off all their energy,
While, with some fur friends, they find synergy.

11

Experts at investigations,
Safeguarding for generations,
These agents protect and defend,
So in peace our time we do spend.

College training and preparatory,
All for academic gain and glory,
A private and elite institution,
Young minds are the future contribution.

A 1920s mansion of splendor,
Where heads of state visited its grandeur.
Be a member of this private club now;
You can hold your event and say a vow.

14

Need for speed or a unique event space?
Here's the place, get ready to race,
Do your rounds in these electric go-karts,
Or practice ax throwing, if you've the heart.

15

1.1 million square feet of shopping,
You can plan to go 'til you're dropping,
All these great stores exist in one great place,
A weather-free and fully indoor space.

16

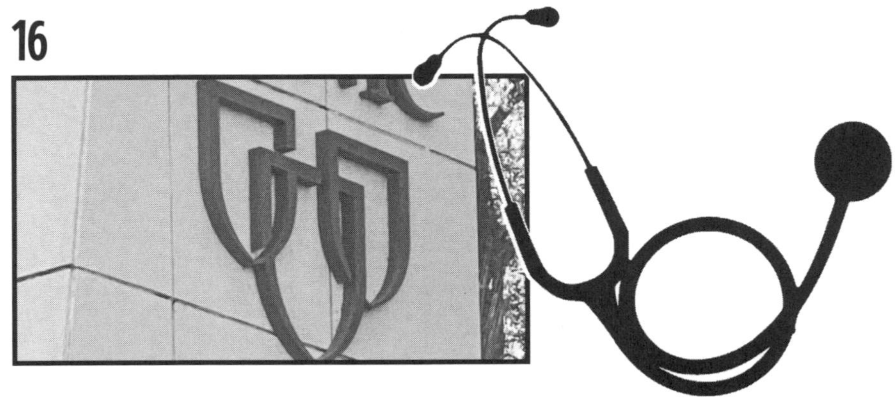

The best place for those who're hard to treat,
Folks come from afar for doctors to meet,
State-of-the-art healing technology,
Care from cardiac to oncology.

17

If you seek a soccer or football game,
Head to this park and you might find the same.
Here's where the regional teams meet,
Cheer on your child their rival to beat.

18

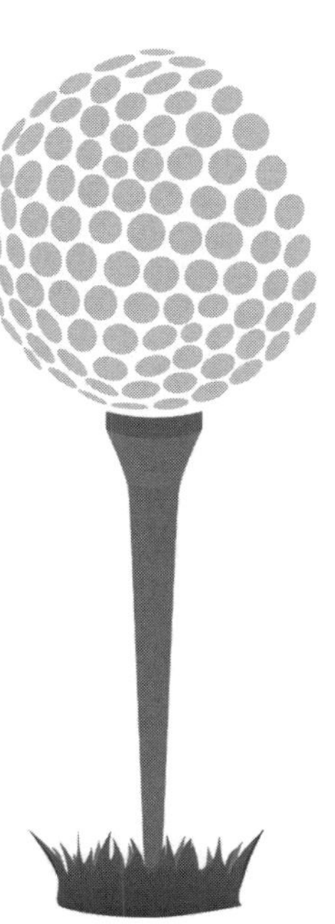

It's a multinational sports compound,
Here, generational fun is found,
Line up to play on their multi-deck,
Follow the screen as your ball it does check.

19

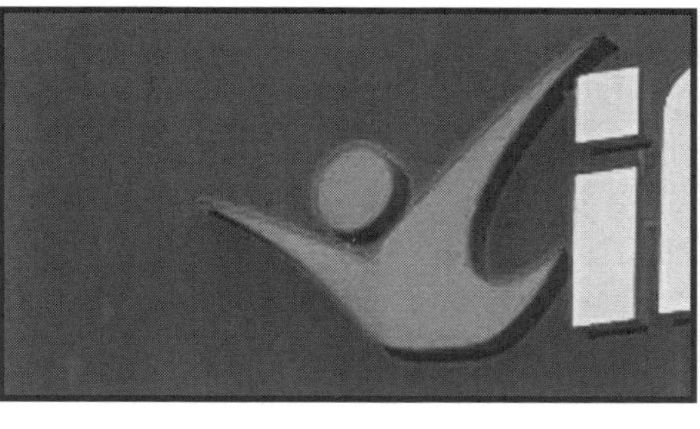

If you seek thrills but are fearful of heights,
This location has solved your plight.
For this adventure you'll get to soar,
Flip and float and never hit the floor.

Mandarin

Drive

Named for the mandarin orange, this neighborhood is a quiet suburban community with stunning views of the St. Johns River's east bank. Author Harriet Beecher Stowe of *Uncle Tom's Cabin* once lived here, along with famous artist Lee Adams, whose work reflects inspiration from the area. Delightful green space, historical landmarks, and exciting dining can be found in this Bold City treasure.

1

There's a bit for everyone here,
Trails and a boat ramp: grab your gear,
Go and see the nature center
When today, at last, you enter.

2

Be transported through sands of time
When at last this old place you find,
What can we learn from these structures,
About history and its cultures?

3

In this building was once a school
Founded by a famous jewel,
Who authored a book that's known still,
About the strength of human will.

4

For children in Mandarin who play ball,
This park's the stop, with plenty of sprawl,
A gift from a family who was kind,
Gave a future generation a find.

5

Generations have been laid to rest here,
Circa 1800, the stones are clear,
The stories could easily fill a book
From every corner and every nook.

6

Just plain lovely, located off Hood,
This green space knows how to be good,
America's pastime, soccer, and more,
Hundreds of acres your enjoyment for.

____

____

7

Perhaps the most unique eats in J-town,
Worth a visit even if you cross town,
Look out for the taxidermy stockpile,
Meander around, it might take a while.

____

____

8

They can trace their roots back through 10 decades,
When times were changing, and so were the trades,
The mission was clear, yes, right from the start,
Serve others with love, yes, right from the heart.

9

Where the mustangs are wild and free,
That is where the youth want to be,
Lacrosse, bowling, and volleyball,
There's a team for any and all.

10

For six great decades, the faithful have come
To seek out some peace, grace, and wisdom from
The trials of this earth, and the stress that weighs,
To serve with kindness, and forgive foul ways.

Orange Park

Drive

Orange Park is a town that lies in the suburbs of Jacksonville, west of Mandarin across the St. Johns River. Featuring a unique history of its own, an Orange Park visit will include lovely riverfront views, historical parks, and plenty of family-friendly fun.

1

A brand-new playground, a very old plot,
We'd like to remember a time forgot,
Tour the old structures to remember, then,
The ages before, and what could have been.

2

American diner fare at its best
When fulfilling your hunger is the quest,
Hearty portions and quality dishes,
Breakfast and lunch options for your wishes.

3

Care for some blackjack or maybe poker?
Cast your wager, do not be a joker.
Sushi and burgers, tasty food and drink,
Even simulcast a play you can sink.

4

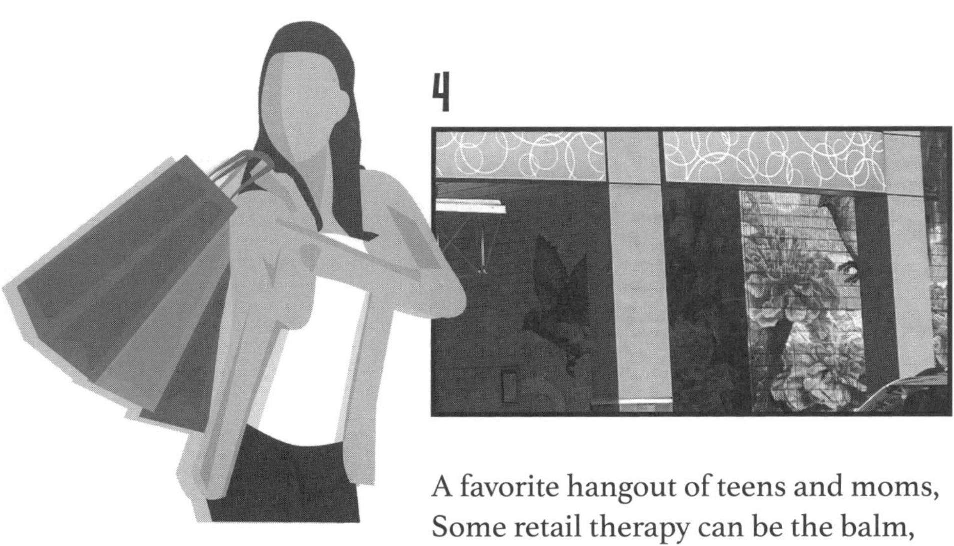

A favorite hangout of teens and moms,
Some retail therapy can be the balm,
Just hang out, swing by the food court,
A visit is fun, whether long or short.

5

The heir of Palmolive's old winter home
Now is a luxury space you can roam.
Whether you stay, or rent as a venue,
I think you'll enjoy all on the menu.

Just north of Orange Park, this green space is poised,
Tucked in the suburbs, away from the noise,
You can play some ball or maybe grill out,
Memories are made here in the dugout.

For four generations, they've laid to rest
Our lost family and those put to test,
Comfort and compassion do guide the way
For the occasion of that solemn day.

8

More than four generations have gone ere,
Bringing their own style of personal flair,
"Go, Raiders" is their official motto:
Say it loud, with even more vibrato.

9

Open to the public, and it is free,
This is the place all the kids want to be.
You must wear a helmet, please remember,
The tricks are fun, even in December.